COLOR KNITTING
with Confidence

COLOR KNITTING

with Confidence

Unlock the Secrets of Fair Isle, Intarsia, and More
with 30 Vibrant Colorwork Techniques

Nguyen Le

A QUINTET BOOK

First edition for the United States and Canada published in 2014 by
Barron's Educational Series, Inc.

All inquiries should be addressed to:
Barron's Educational Series, Inc.
250 Wireless Boulevard
Hauppauge, NY 11788
www.barronseduc.com

ISBN: 978-1-4380-0424-2
Library of Congress Control Number: 2014941848

QTT.CWCO

Conceived, designed, and produced by:
Quintet Publishing
4th Floor, Sheridan House
114-116 Western Road
Hove BN3 1DD
United Kingdom

Project Editor: Caroline Elliker
Designer: Bonnie Bryan
Photographer: Lydia Evans
Art Director: Michael Charles
Editorial Director: Emma Bastow
Publisher: Mark Searle

Manufactured in China by 1010 Printing International Ltd.

9 8 7 6 5 4 3 2 1

5 Scissors

A pair of small, sharp scissors is an essential tool for cutting steeks precisely, and for trimming loose yarn ends.

6 Stitch Markers

Stitch markers are useful for counting stitches and pattern repeats, as well as marking the beginning of a round in circular knitting. Most are designed as rings that are placed over the knitting needle when working in the round.

7 Tape Measure and Ruler

Some projects call for knitting for a certain length, and rulers and tape measures come in handy for measuring your progress. I like a 60 in. (152 cm) tape marked with inches and centimeters on either side.

8 Tapestry Needle

Tapestry needles come in various sizes. For knitted fabrics, the eye needs to be large enough to accommodate the yarn, and the point should be relatively blunt.

9 Yarn Stranding Guide

Yarn stranding guides are made from plastic or wire, and slide over your finger to sit just above your knuckle. The have separators to hold two yarns and keep them separated to prevent tangles while you're knitting colorwork.

10 Yarn Bobbins

Yarn bobbins are used in intarsia knitting to hold small lengths of yarn neatly. They come in different shapes and sizes, and are usually a flat piece of plastic that the yarn is wound onto. You can make your own using a piece of cardboard or heavy cardstock: Cut two slits, one to anchor the yarn, and the other to hold the other end in place. Unwind enough yarn for each section as you work. You can also make yarn butterflies to keep your yarns organized (see page 67).

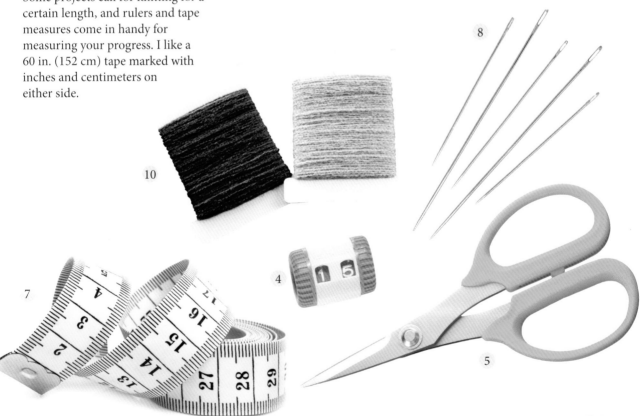

Types of Yarn for Colorwork

There are many different yarn types and colors, but you can't go wrong with a decent wool blend.

Essentially any yarn can be used in colorwork, but wool or wool blends work the best. Wool has an elasticity and grip, so it's forgiving and doesn't slide around on the needles as much as other yarns. It will also fall into place and smooth out like butter when blocked—an essential finishing technique for colorwork knitting. Keep in mind that superwash wool is different than normal wool. Superwash wool goes through a chemical process that strips the "scales" from the wool, which gives it its grip. But because the scales are stripped, it prevents the yarn from being felted when washed in the machine, which is a major plus for baby knits. Feel free to substitute yarns for any of the projects in this book. Use the same weight of yarn as used in the project, and be sure to knit a swatch to match the gauge.

How to Read Charts

Charts enable you to visualize the end result, so learning to read them is an important part of color knitting.

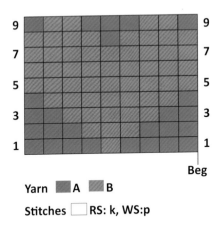

Yarn ▨ A ▨ B
Stitches ☐ RS: k, WS:p

Charts are gridded color blocks that can show allover patterns, a section of repeats, or a single motif in one area, such as in intarsia patterns. Instructions indicate when to begin following the chart. This example is taken from the Detachable Collar project on page 72.

Charts show the right side of the pattern. They have symbols and a key to decipher the instructions. Usually, each block represents one stitch and the color of that stitch. In double knitting patterns with mirrored images, each block represents two stitches. Charts begin at the bottom right-hand corner. For flat knitting, the first row is read from right to left for right side rows. The next row above is a wrong side row, and is read from left to right. In circular knitting, every row is a right side row, and charts are read from right to left for every row.

Knitting Abbreviations

alt	alternate	**psso**	pass slipped stitch over	**WS**	wrong side
beg	begin(s)/beginning	**p2sso**	pass two slipped sts over	**wyib**	with yarn in back
BO	bind off	**p2tog**	purl two stitches together	**wyif**	with yarn in front
CC	contrasting color	**pm**	place marker	**yfwd**	yarn forward
cn	cable needle	**prev**	previous	**yo**	yarn over
cont	continue	**pwise**	purlwise	**yon**	yarn over needle
CO	cast on	**rem**	remain/remaining	**yrn**	yarn around needle
dec	decrease(s)/decreasing	**rep**	repeat(s)	⋆	repeat from starting point (i.e., repeat from ⋆)
DPN(s)	double pointed needle(s)	**rev St st**	reverse stockinette stitch		
foll	follow(s)/following	**RH**	right hand		
inc	increase(s)/increasing	**RS**	right side		
k	knit	**RHN**	right-hand needle		
k2tog	knit two stitches	**rnd(s)**	round(s)		
K1f&b	knit into front and back of stitch	**RSF**	right side facing		
kwise	knitwise	**sk**	skip		
LH	left hand	**sl**	slip		
LHN	left-hand needle	**sl1k**	slip one knitwise		
lp(s)	loop(s)	**sl1p**	slip one purlwise		
M1	make 1 stitch	**sl st**	slip stitch		
M1L	make 1 left slanting stitch	**ssk**	slip, slip, knit these two stitches together—a decrease		
M1R	make 1 right slanting stitch				
MC	main color	**st(s)**	stitch(es)		
p	purl	**St st**	stockinette stitch		
patt	pattern(s)	**tbl**	through back loop		

UK/US Conversions

UK	US
Aran	Fisherman
cast off	bind off
cotton wool	absorbent cotton
double moss stitch	moss stitch
lengthways	lengthwise
single moss stitch	seed stitch
stocking stitch	stockinette stitch
tension	gauge
visible increase	bar increase

Casting On

Making a Slip Knot
Casting on is the first step in hand knitting and it provides the first row of loops on the needle. The first step is to make a slip knot.

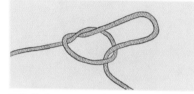

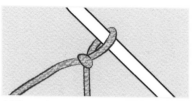

1 Holding the yarn in both hands, make a small loop in the yarn. Take the piece you are holding in your right hand underneath the loop.

2 Pull this piece of yarn through the original loop, to create a knot. Do not pull the short end of the yarn through the loop.

3 Place the slip knot onto the knitting needle.

Cable Method
The diagrams below show the cable method. The cable cast-on creates a firm yet elastic edge ideal for use on ribbed edges

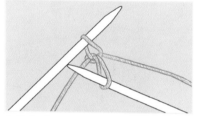

1 Place the slip knot onto the knitting needle and hold the needle in your left hand. Slide the right-hand knitting needle through the loop created by the slip knot from front to back.

2 With your right hand, wrap the yarn around the right-hand knitting needle counterclockwise from back to front.

3 Slide the right-hand needle through the loop on the left-hand needle, catching the wrapped yarn and bringing it through the loop to create another loop.

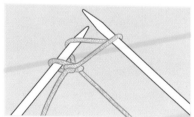

4 Pass the left-hand needle over the top of the new loop, placing the tip of the needle through the loop on the right-hand needle. Remove the right-hand needle, transferring the stitch to the left-hand needle.

5 Make each subsequent stitch by placing the right-hand needle between the last two stitches made on the left-hand needle, and repeating Steps 2–4.

In English-style (Cable Method) knitting, the needle with the stitches to be worked is held in the left hand and the yarn is held in the right; the yarn is wrapped around the needles to make the stitches. In continental knitting, the yarn and needle with the stitches to be worked are both held in the left hand; the yarn is then "picked up" to make stitches. The end results are the same, it just depends on what feels comfortable to you.

Continental Method

The continental method, also called the long-tail or double cast-on method, is ideal for beginners and creates a stable, flexible edge. You need to leave a tail approximately 3–5 times as long as the desired cast-on edge when you use this method.

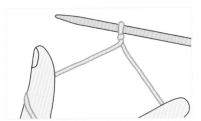

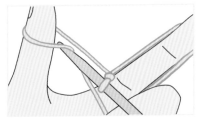

1 Make a slip knot, leaving the correct length of tail, and place on the right-hand needle. Grab both ends of the yarn in your hand, with the long tail on the left and the ball end to the right. Place the thumb and index finger of your left hand between the yarn ends so that the working yarn is around your forefinger and the tail end is around your thumb, making a diamond shape with the yarn.

2 Pull the needle downward to create a "heart" shape with the yarn. Bring needle up through the loop on the thumb from the bottom.

3 Draw the loop from the thumb up and grab a strand from around the forefinger with the needle.

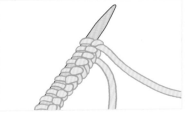

4 Draw loop from forefinger back down through the loop on the thumb to create a stitch on the needle.

5 Drop loop off thumb and, placing thumb back through center of the two strands of yarn in the diamond configuration, tighten the resulting stitch on needle. Rep Steps 2–7 until you have desired number of stitches.

Binding Off

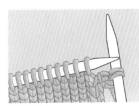

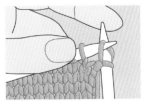

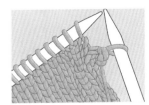

1 At the point where you are ready to bind off, knit the first two stitches.

2 Slip the left-hand needle into the first stitch on the right-hand needle, and lift it over the second stitch and off the needle.

3 Knit the next stitch so that there are two stitches on the right-hand needle again.

4 Repeat Steps 2 and 3 until all stitches are knitted from the left-hand needle and one stitch remains on right-hand needle. Make the last stitch loop larger, break the yarn, and draw firmly through the last stitch to fasten off.

Knit and Purl Stitches

Most knitting is based on combinations of just two basic stitches—knit stitch and purl stitch.

Knit Stitch

  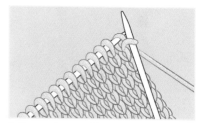

1 Hold the needle with the stitches to be knitted in the left hand and with the yarn behind the work.

2 Insert the right-hand needle into the first stitch from front to back. Take the yarn over it, forming a loop.

3 Bring the needle and the new loop to the front of the work through the stitch, and slide the original stitch off the left-hand needle.

Purl Stitch

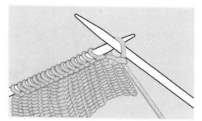 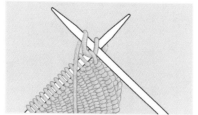 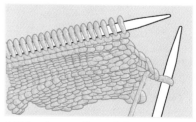

1 Hold the stitches to be purled in the left hand, with the yarn at the front of the work.

2 Insert the right-hand needle through the front of the stitch, from right to left. Take the yarn over and under, forming a loop.

3 Take the needle and the new loop through the back and slide the stitch off the left-hand needle.

Basic Knitting Stitch Variations

Garter Stitch

If you were to work rows of just knit, or just purl stitches in succession, you would create a knitted fabric known as garter stitch. This looks the same on both sides of the fabric.

Stockinette Stitch

To make a fabric using stockinette stitch, work rows of knit stitches and rows of purl stitches alternately. Stockinette stitch fabric is different on both sides. The right side is smooth, and you will be able to see that the stitches create a zigzag effect. The wrong side is bumpy and looks a little like garter stitch.

Seed Stitch (or Moss Stitch)

Seed stitch fabric looks like tiny little seeds across the fabric. It is made by knitting one stitch and purling the next stitch alternately across the right side of the fabric. On the wrong side, knit the purls and purl the knits, and continue doing so for every stitch.

Decreasing

Decreasing is a shaping technique used to make the fabric narrower by reducing the number of stitches. Various techniques are used, depending on whether the decrease needs to slope to the left or the right.

Sloping to the Right

Knit Two Together (k2tog)

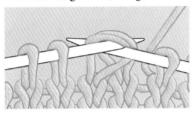

1 Slide the right-hand needle through the second and then the first stitches on the left-hand needle from front to back. Wrap the yarn around the right-hand needle as for a normal knit stitch.

2 Knit the two stitches together as if knitting normally and slide both off the left-hand needle.

Purl Two Together (p2tog)

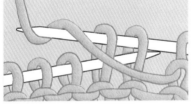

1 Slide the right-hand needle through the first two stitches on the left-hand needle "purlwise."

2 Purl the two stitches together as if purling normally and slide both off the left-hand needle.

Gauge

Gauge is the number of stitches and rows per inch in a knitted fabric. Knitting a gauge swatch to match your pattern gauge is important in ensuring that the finished project will be the correct size. To knit a gauge swatch, work in the same type of stitch as the pattern for accurate results. You can simply knit a 4-inch square, or knit a garter stitch border around the perimeter of the 4-inch square for flatter edges. Because tension varies from person to person, you may need to try other needle sizes than the one suggested. Change your needle size up or down to match the pattern gauge as necessary. It is also important to block your swatch as you would for the finished project, before measuring stitches for an accurate count. Use a ruler or gauge measurement tool, which has an L-shaped cutout to measure horizontally for stitches, and vertically for rows.

Sloping to the Left

Slip Slip Knit (ssk)

1 To decrease knitwise, slip 2 stitches from the left-hand needle to the right-hand needle.

2 Insert the tip of the left-hand needle from left to right through the front loop of both stitches.

3 Knit the stitches together from this position.

Increasing

Increases are used to make the fabric wider by increasing the number of stitches. This is usually worked by knitting into the back of the bar between stitches. It is a neat increase worked between two stitches.

M1R (make one right slanting) Front

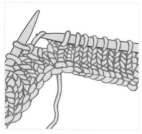 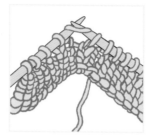 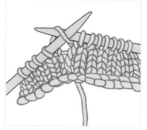 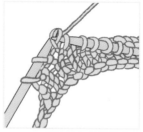

1 Pass the right-hand knitting needle underneath the "bar" of yarn between two stitches from front to back.

2 Slip the loop onto the left-hand needle and remove the right-hand needle.

3 Knit into the back of the loop to twist it, by inserting the right-hand needle behind the yarn on the left-hand needle from right to left.

4 Finish the stitch as a normal knit stitch, remove the left-hand needle, passing the new stitch onto the right-hand needle.

M1R (make one right slanting) Back

1 Pass the right-hand knitting needle underneath the "bar" of yarn between two stitches from back to front.

2 Slip the loop onto the left-hand needle and remove the right-hand needle.

3 Purl into the front loop to twist it, by inserting the right-hand needle behind the yarn on the left-hand needle from right to left.

4 Finish the stitch as a normal purl stitch, remove the left-hand needle, passing the new stitch onto the right-hand needle.

M1L (make 1 left slanting) Front

1 Pass the right-hand knitting needle underneath the "bar" of yarn between two stitches from back to front.

2 Slip the loop onto the left-hand needle and remove the right-hand needle.

3 Knit into the front loop to twist it, by inserting the right-hand needle behind the yarn on the left-hand needle from left to right.

4 Finish as a normal knit stitch, remove the left-hand needle, passing the new stitch onto the right-hand needle.

M1L (make 1 left slanting) Back

1 Pass the right-hand knitting needle underneath the "bar" of yarn between two stitches from front to back.

2 Slip the loop onto the left-hand needle and remove the right-hand needle.

3 Purl into the back loop to twist it, by inserting the right-hand needle behind the yarn on the left-hand needle from left to right.

4 Finish as a normal purl stitch, remove the left-hand needle, passing the new stitch onto the right-hand needle.

Knitting in the Round with Double-Pointed Needles
Divide the stitches evenly between three or four of the needles and, once the cast-on row has been made, use the fourth/fifth needle to knit. Ensure the cast-on row is not twisted before you start knitting and use a stitch marker to identify the first stitch. Once all the stitches from one needle have been knitted, use the free needle to work the stitches from the next needle. Keep the gauge (tension) of the stitches consistent when transferring from one needle to another; always draw the yarn up firmly when knitting the first stitch at the change-over point to avoid a ladder or loopy stitch.

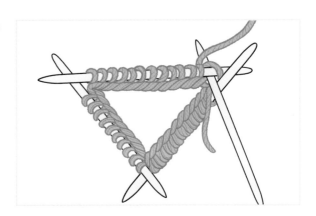

Finishing

Weaving in Ends

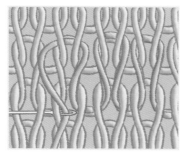

1 Thread yarn through loops along the edge for 1½–2 in. (4–5 cm), then secure by sewing back through a few of the last loops.

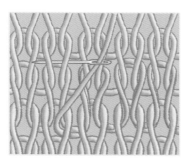

2 Pass the end through the stitches, inserting the needle from the top of the loop on the first, then the bottom on the next alternately for about 1½–2 in. (4–5 cm), then sew back through a few of the last loops to secure.

Kitchener Stitch (Grafting)

This technique was originally used to graft sock toes, but it is fabulous for many different seams. Any two pieces of knitting that have been left on the needles rather than bound off can be grafted together with "Kitchener stitch" (sometimes called mattress stitch) for an invisible seam.

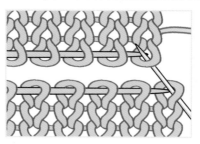

1 Using the yarn, work from right to left. From the back of the fabric, bring the needle through the first stitch of the lower fabric, and the first stitch of the upper fabric.

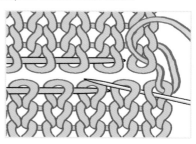

2 From the front, thread the needle back through the center of the first stitch on the lower fabric where the yarn leaves, then out of the center of the next stitch on the left.

3 Thread the needle through the center of the top stitch and along the center of the next. Continue like this and, as each stitch is worked, keep slipping the knitting needle from them.

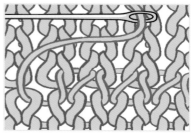

4 Continue like this to complete the seam.

Duplicate Stitch
This stitch is a way to add a little color to a piece.

1 Thread a length of yarn through a tapestry needle and pull the needle up from back to front through the center bottom point of a knit V stitch.

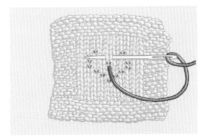

2 Pull the needle from right to left under the bottom legs of the stitch above the one you're duplicating. Pull the yarn gently through.

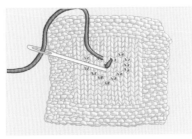

3 Pull the needle back down into the first hole from front to back. You've completed one duplicate stitch.

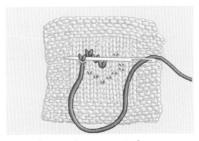

4 Work into the next stitches you want to duplicate, until you've finished the design.

Blocking
Blocking is a finishing technique that helps shape your knitted pieces and smooth out the stitches before sewing them together.

Start by pinning your piece to a blocking board to the correct size. (I use my ironing board for small pieces in a pinch). You can use the steam from an iron to hover over and steam block your pieces, or you can pin and spritz your piece with a bit of water and let it air dry.

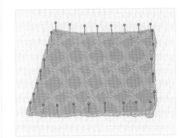

I-cord
The I-cord is a tube knitted in the round with two double-pointed needles; it is a quick and easy way of making a versatile cord (see Purse on page 64).

To work a cord successfully, cast on 3–5 stitches. Knit to the end of the row—do not turn, slide the stitches back up to the right-hand point of the needle. Insert the needle in your right hand into the first stitch, bring the yarn from the left-hand side and knit to the end of the row. Keep repeating this process until the required length of cord is achieved. Bind off as you would normally, or thread the end of the yarn through all the stitches on the needle and pull tight.

All About Color

ONCE YOU'VE MASTERED YOUR KNITS AND PURLS, IT'S TIME TO LEARN ABOUT COLOR MATCHING SO THAT YOU CAN CREATE MORE ATTRACTIVE DESIGNS USING THE STITCHES YOU KNOW.

Anyone who's stepped into a yarn store knows the feeling of excitement from seeing the rows upon rows of color choices. With so many options, trying to select colors for a project can be quite daunting. That's where *Color Knitting with Confidence* steps in to guide you. Of course, everyone has their own color preferences, or colors that they gravitate toward more than others, and it's important to remember that there are no wrong color combinations. Different pairs or groups of colors will give a different feel to a project, and it's up to you to decide what effect you'd like. Whether it's bright and popping, or soft and subtle, choose colors that make you (or the lucky recipient) happy, because it's you (or them) who's going to enjoy it.

Describing Color

The color wheel is comprised of twelve colors, and traditionally begins with yellow at the top and the following colors clockwise from yellow are: yellow-orange, orange, red-orange, red, red-violet, violet, blue-violet, blue, blue-green, green, and yellow-green. Color can be described in three main ways—by hue, value, and saturation, which we'll explore below.

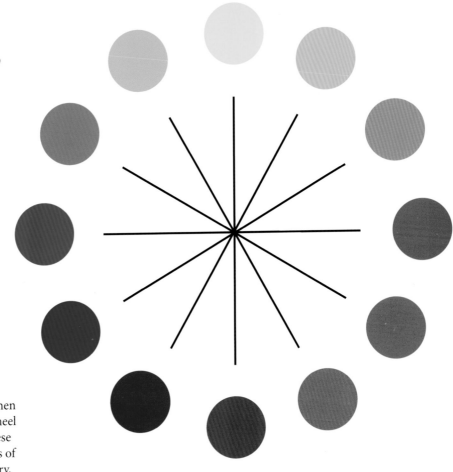

Hue

Hue refers to the actual color, such as red, yellow, blue, or purple. It's what we think of when we think of color. The color wheel shows a collection of hues. These hues are broken up into groups of colors called primary, secondary, and tertiary colors.

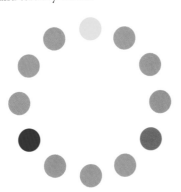

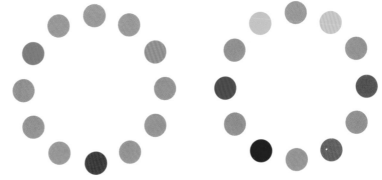

Primary Colors

Primary colors consist of red, yellow, and blue. They are the first colors, and are mixed to create all other colors on the wheel.

Secondary Colors

Secondary colors are created when two primary colors are equally mixed together. Red and blue make violet, red and yellow make orange, and blue and yellow make green.

Tertiary Colors

Tertiary colors are created when one primary color is mixed with a secondary color. Red and orange make red-orange, orange and yellow make yellow-orange, yellow and green make yellow-green, and so on.

Value

Value describes the lightness or darkness of a color. It can be difficult to determine the value of a color, because the hue is the first thing we usually see. To better understand it, imagine a gray scale similar to that below. It shows all the shades of gray from white to black—light to dark. Value also refers to the amount of contrast between hues, which is important in colorwork, because it affects how the pattern is perceived. High contrast colors will show a clearer stitch pattern, while lower contrast colors will produce a more subtle stitch pattern.

Saturation

Saturation describes the amount of pure hue in a color. When a color is mixed with white, gray, or black, it becomes a tint, tone, or shade—a light, medium, or dark version of that color. The color becomes less saturated as a tint, medium saturated as a tone, and more deeply saturated as a shade. The intensity of a color is determined by the amount of white, gray, or black it is mixed with, as demonstrated on the right.

Color Combinations

The color wheel is a great tool for selecting harmonious colors—groups of colors that are pleasing to the eye.

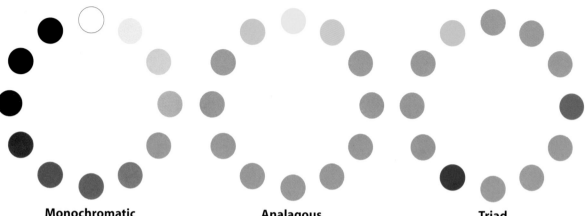

Monochromatic
Tints, tones, and/or shades of just one hue. Ombres are a great example of this, and create a lovely soft effect.

Analagous
Any three colors next to each other on the color wheel.

Triad
A set of three colors proportionally spaced apart on the color wheel. The primary colors (red, yellow and blue) are an example of triad colors.

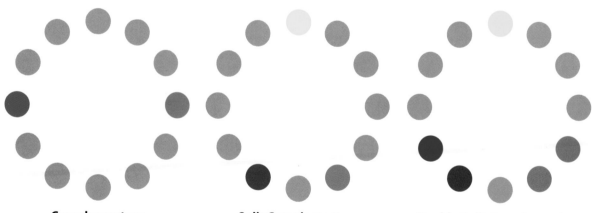

Complementary
Colors that are directly across each other on the color wheel. Because they are opposites, they create a lot of excitement when used together.

Split Complementary
A set of three colors—a color and one color on either side of its complement.

Double Split Complementary
A set of five colors—a color and two colors on either side of its complement.

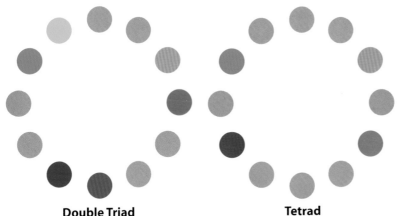

Double Triad
A set of six colors—two sets of triads.

Tetrad
A set of four colors that form a rectangle on the color wheel.

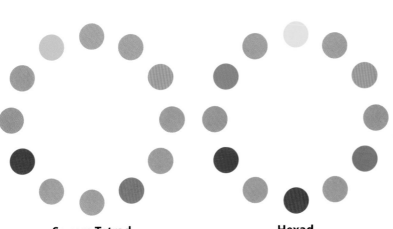

Square Tetrad
A set of four colors that form a square on the color wheel.

Hexad
A set of six colors that form a hexagon on the color wheel. They are three sets of complementary colors, and there are only two possible hexads on the wheel.

Color Temperature
Colors can also be described as warm or cool. Cooler colors tend to recede, and warmer colors tend to extend forward. Half the color wheel is warm colors, and the other half is cool colors. Yellow through red-violet are warm colors and violet through yellow-green are cool colors. Using the hues from one side creates an easily compatible color palette.

Cool

Warm

Striped Knitting

STACK ROW AFTER ROW OF COLOR BY KNITTING WITH STRIPES. IT'S ONE OF THE SIMPLEST COLORWORK TECHNIQUES AND USES TWO OR MORE COLORS THAT ARE CHANGED AT THE END OF A ROW OR ROUND.

Although it's a basic technique, knitted stripes make engaging and dynamic pieces. By playing with color combinations and the number of rows between each change, you can create subtle or bold outcomes. Graduating monochromatic colors generate a soft ombre, while using hues directly opposite each other on the color wheel create an exciting and stimulating effect.

Stripes can also be incorporated with just about any stitch pattern—stockinette, garter, basketweave, cables, ribbing—to name a few. You'll see how differently stripes behave with each pattern, which can make for very interesting sequences.

Tips

- Use opposites on the color wheel for a striking effect.
- Stripes are versatile so experiment with different stitches.
- Use stripes to create a graduated effect.

First Steps

Joining New Yarn

New colors are always joined at the beginning of a row or round. In flat knitting, stripes are knit in pairs or even-numbered sections so color changes happen along the same edge, leaving fewer yarn ends to weave in.

Carrying Yarn

In most cases, if colors are repeated in the stripe pattern, they can be carried up along one edge, eliminating the need to weave in yarn ends after each color change. And if knitting in the round, the same idea applies—yarns are carried up at the beginning of the round along the wrong side and twisted together before beginning the next color.

1 Twist new color underneath previous color.

2 Twisting yarns tend to fall to the back side. Here you can see both colors carried up along the edge.

1

2

Knitting Stripes in the Round

When knitting stripes in the round, you'll notice that the end of the stripe won't match up perfectly with the beginning. There are a couple ways to work the first stitch after a stripe to make a smoother transition. These techniques require at least 2 rounds of the same color. If you have just one round of stripe, usually you can wiggle your knitting a little and the jog will even out.

1 Here, the stripe is knit as normal in the round, and has a noticeable jog.

2 Knitting into the stitch below is one way to hide a jog. Knit one round as normal in the new color. At the beginning of the second round, lift the stitch below onto the left hand needle with the stitch above it and knit the 2 stitches together.

3 Slipping stitches is another way to hide a jog. It elongates the stitch, evening it out with stripe. Knit one round as normal in the new color. Slip the first stitch of the round and knit as normal.

1

2

3

Yarn Tails

There are a few ways to deal with yarn tails in striped knitting, and in colorwork knitting in general.

- Weave in tails one at a time on the back of your work, moving back and then forth to hide and secure the yarn (see page 18).

- As you knit, weave in yarn tails to minimize the amount of work in the end. Do this by laying the tail alternately over and under the working yarn on the back of your work, as you knit.

- If your piece calls for a fringe, incorporate the yarn tails into the fringe tails.

Pennant Garland,
see page 42

Sample Stitch Patterns with Stripes

Stripes can look very different depending on the stitch pattern they're used with. They can be very clear and crisp, or blended in. Here are a few common stitch patterns and how they appear using stripes.

Stockinette Stitch

This is probably the most common stitch used with stripes. Alternating knit and purl rows creates a stockinette fabric. The colors here are changed every two rows. On the front, the lines are smooth, neat, and clearly defined. The back, also known as reverse stockinette, shows bumpier edges, and less even spacing between the colors.

Garter Stitch

This stitch is created by knitting every row, and makes a stretchy flat fabric that doesn't curl. When using only one color, garter stitch also creates a reversible fabric. Incorporating stripes into garter stitch makes each side looks different. The colors here are changed every two rows, and you can see the difference from front to back. The front has very clean lines, and the back also has straight lines, but their placement shows more bumps and ridges.

Front

Front

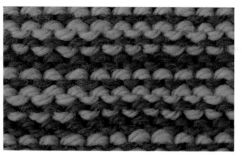

Back

Back

Rib Stitch

The rib stitch is created by alternating knits and purls evenly across a row and then knitting the knits and purling the purls on subsequent rows. The number of alternating stitches can be different for ribbing. For example, k1, p1 is a 1x1 rib, k2, p2 is a 2x2 rib, and k3, p3 is a 3x3 rib. These samples use a 2x2 rib and show two ways that stripes can be knit into ribbing.

In the top image (figure 1), stripes are worked in the rib pattern for each color change, and both sides of the fabric are the same. You can see the how the line of the stripes breaks up on the purl stitches and doesn't continue across as smoothly, which is perfectly fine.

In the image in figure 2, the first row of each color change is knit all the way across, and then the rest of the stripe is knit as normal in the ribbing. This knit row is virtually invisible and creates a crisp straight line on the front side, and an interesting stripe pattern on the back (figure 3).

Figure 1

Figure 2

Figure 3

Baby Blanket

A lovely, sunny ombre baby blanket that's sure to brighten up any nursery. It's quick and simple to make, using monochromatic blocks of color. Yarns for each section are broken with the start of a new color, and can be woven in as you knit, or at the very end.

Materials

- Brown Sheep Lamb's Pride Superwash Bulky, 100 % wool, 3.5 oz (100 g), 110 yds (101 m)
  1 skein of each in the following shades:
  A; 125, Goldenrod
  B; 305, Impasse Yellow
  C; 307, Lullaby
  D; 730, Natural
  E; 740, Snow

Needles and Notions

- US 10½ (6.5 mm) circular needle, 32 in. (80 cm) length
- Tapestry needle

Pattern Notes

This blanket is worked in five blocks with twenty-seven rows of each color and a color change on the twenty-eighth row worked as a reverse stockinette row. This technique means to work "knit" stitches on the wrong side of the fabric to show purl bumps on the right side. Notice how the reverse stockinette breaks up what would normally be a smooth line of color change. Eight rows of garter stitch line the bottom and top of the blanket with a six-stitch garter border on the right- and left-hand side of the blanket. Use either side of the blanket as shown.

Instructions

With A, cast on 88 sts.
Rows 1-9: knit every row.
Row 10 (WS): k6, p to last 6 sts, k6.
Row 11 (RS): knit.
Rows 12-27: rep Rows 10 and 11.
Row 28 (WS): break A, join B and knit.
Row 29: knit.
Row 30-55: rep Rows 10 and 11.
Row 56 (WS): break B, join C and knit.
Row 57: knit.
Rows 58-83: rep Rows 10 and 11.
Row 84 (WS): break C, join D and knit.
Row 85: knit.

Rows 86-111: rep Rows 10 and 11
Row 112 (WS): break D, join E and knit.
Row 113: knit.
Rows 114-131: rep Rows 10 and 11.
Rows 132-139: knit every row.
Bind off all sts.
Weave in ends and block to finished dimensions.

Sizing

Gauge
14 sts and 18 rows to 4 in. (10 cm) over St st
Finished dimensions
25 x 30 in. (63.5 x 76 cm)

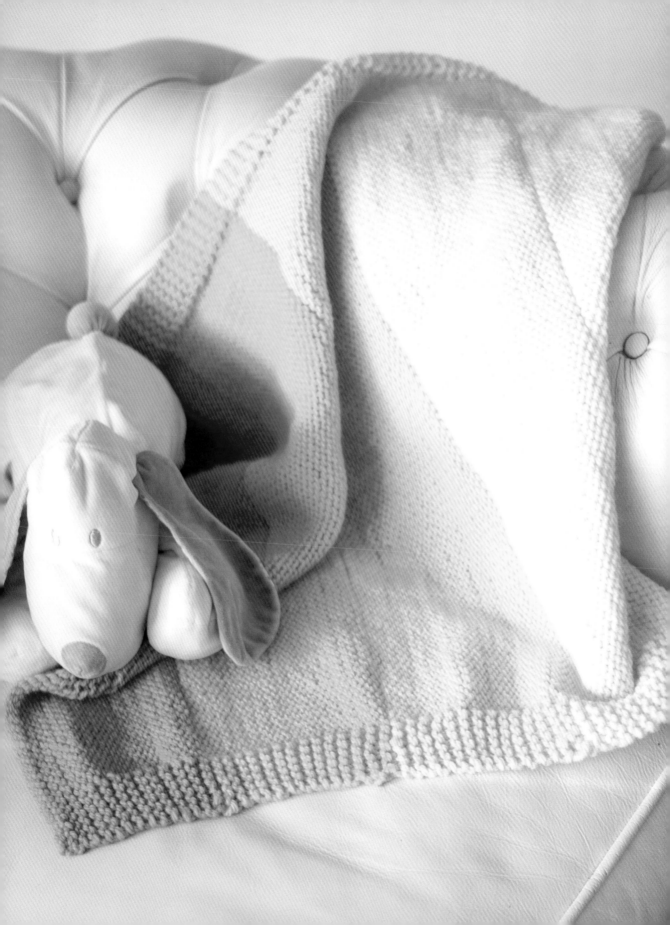

Baby Bib

This mini kerchief works as a great little bib for baby. A simple stripe pattern uses increases to form this hip little triangle. It is worked from the top down, beginning at the center top, and fans out as the stitches are increased. See how the increases moving down the center change the lines of the stripes to form a V-shape instead of moving straight across. This is a great way to play with stripes.

Materials

- Brown Sheep Cotton Fleece, 80% cotton, 20% merino wool, 3.5 oz (100 g), 215 yds (197 m) 1 skein of each in the following shades:
  A; CW-767, Hawaiian Sky
  B; CW-345, Gold Dust

Needles and Notions

- US 6 (4 mm) knitting needles
- G/4 (4 mm) crochet hook
- Stitch markers
- ½ in. (1.25 cm) button
- Tapestry needle

Pattern Notes

Carry yarn loosely up the side for each color change.

Sizing

Gauge
22 sts and 28 rows to 4 in. (10 cm) over St st

Finished dimensions
15 x 8 in. (38 x 20.5 cm)

Instructions

Set-up
With A, cast on 3 sts.
Row 1 (WS): knit.
Row 2 (RS): k1, m1R, k1, m1L, k1. (5 sts)
Row 3: knit.
Row 4: k2, m1R, pm, k1, pm, m1L, k2. (7 sts)
Row 5: knit.
Row 6: k3, m1R, sm, k1, sm, m1L, k3. (9 sts)
Row 7: k3, p1, sm, p1, sm, p1, k3.

Stripe pattern with 3-st garter border on both sides
Row 8 (RS): join B, k3, m1L, k1, m1R, sm, k1, sm, m1L, k1, m1R, k3. (13 sts)
Row 9 (WS): k3, p3, sm, sl1, sm, p3, k3.

Row 10: join A, k3, m1L, k to marker, m1R, sm, k1, sm, m1L, k to last 3 sts, m1R, k3. (17 sts)
Row 11: k3, p to marker, sm, sl1, sm, p to last 3 sts, k3.
Rep Rows 10 and 11 another 19 times, alternating colors A and B every 2 rows, ending with color B.

Garter edge
Next row (RS): with A, rep Row 10.
Next row (WS): knit.
Rep last 2 rows twice more.
Bind off loosely but do not fasten off last st.
Slip st to crochet hook, ch 10 and, using the tapestry needle, secure end to make a fastening loop at the right-hand corner.

Finishing
Weave in all loose ends. Block bib to finished dimensions. Sew a button to the left-hand corner.

Striped Bracelet

This diagonal striped bracelet is a new take on a classic friendship bracelet. A quick knit with infinite color combinations, this fun pattern is a great way to practice carrying yarns along an edge.

Materials

- Koigu KPM & KPPPM skeinettes, 100% merino wool, 11 yds (10 m)
  1 skein each of of the following shades:
  A; 1190, Red-orange
  B; 2332, Yellow

Needles and Notions

- US 2 (2.75 mm) knitting needles
- C (2.75 mm) crochet hook
- ½ in. (1.25 cm) button
- Tapestry needle

Sizing

Gauge
Not essential for this project
Finished dimensions
1 x 7 in. (2.5 x 18 cm)

Instructions

With A, cast on 10 sts.
Row 1: knit.
Row 2: sl1, k1, psso, k to last st, m1, k1.
Rows 3 and 4: rep Rows 1 and 2.
Row 5: leaving A attached, join B and knit.
Row 6: using A, rep Row 2.

Rep Rows 1-6 another 8 times, then Rows 1-4 once more. Work more or fewer reps of Rows 1-6 to adjust size for different wrists.
Break B. Bind off loosely with A but do not fasten off last st.
Slip st to crochet hook, ch 16 and, using the tapestry needle, secure end to make a fastening loop at the right-hand corner.

Finishing
Weave in all loose ends.
Block bracelet to finished dimensions.
Using A, sew the button to the opposite end to the fastening loop.

Mail Pocket

Organize your mail with a basketweave wall pocket. Incorporating another stitch into stripes is a great way to add dimension and texture. The pocket is knit in the round from the bottom up, before the top section is worked flat. The addition of a dowel gives a sturdy straight edge for hanging on the wall. When you display it, choose between the seamless color changes on one side, or textured purl ridges on the other.

Sizing

Gauge
20 sts and 30 rows to 4 in. (10 cm) over basketweave st
22 sts and 40 rows to 4 in. (10 cm) over garter st

Finished dimensions
12½ in. (32 cm) tall, 9½ in. (24 cm) wide at the bottom, 10¼ in. (26 cm) wide at the top

Instructions

With A, cast on 88 sts, pm and join for working in the round, taking care not to twist the sts.
Rnd 1: knit.
Rnds 2-7: [k4, p4] rep to end.
Rnd 8: knit.
Rnds 9-13: [p4, k4] rep to end.
Rnd 14: break A, join B and knit.
Rnds 15-19: [k4, p4] rep to end.
Rnd 20: knit.
Rnds 21-25: [p4, k4] rep to end.
Rnd 26: break B, join C and knit.
Rnds 27-31: [k4, p4] rep to end.
Rnd 32: knit.

Rnds 33-37: [p4, k4] rep to end.
Rnd 38: break C, join D and knit.
Rnds 39-43: [k4, p4] rep to end.
Rnd 44: knit.
Rnds 45-49: [p4, k4] rep to end.
Rnd 50: break D, join E and knit.
Rnds 51-55: [k4, p4] rep to end.
Rnd 56: knit.
Rnd 57: purl.
Rnds 58-61: rep Rnds 56 and 57 twice more.
Row 62: bind off 44 sts, k to end. Turn and work flat.
Rows 63-64: knit.
Row 65: break E, join F and knit.

Rows 65-95: knit.
Bind off all sts.

Finishing
Using A and Kitchener stitch, sew the bottom edge together.
Weave in all loose ends.

For an invisible wall hanging, attach the dowel to the top edge. Line up and glue the edge evenly to 2 adjoining sides of the square dowel. Leave to dry. Center and nail the sawtooth picture hanger to the center of the back of the dowel, and hang on the wall.

Pennant Garland

Materials

- Cascade 220 Superwash Sport, 100% superwash merino wool, 1.75 oz (50 g), 136 yds (125 m) 1 skein of each in the following shades:
  A; 827, Coral
  B; 820, Lemon
  C; 826, Tangerine
  D; 802, Green Apple
  E; 1940 Peach

Needles and Notions

- US 5 (3.75 mm) knitting needles
- Tapestry needle
- Twine or string for hanging garland

Pattern Notes

Here are instructions for the basic triangle shape. These triangles are made by decreasing along the edges, so it keeps the stripe moving in a straight line all the way across. Follow the chart to make three different stripe patterns. Knit two of each stripe pattern and flip one of the pair over to show the opposite side, as in the photograph.

Garlands are a wonderfully festive way to decorate for any occasion. This pattern uses small amounts of yarn, and is a perfect way to use up leftover skeins.

Instructions (make 6)

Cast on 26 sts and knit 4 rows in garter st.
Decrease row: k1, sl1, psso, k to last 3 sts, ssk, k1. (2 sts decreased)
Continue in garter st, and rep the decrease row every fourth row until 4 sts remain.
Knit 3 rows.
Next row: k2tog, ssk, and bind off by passing the right hand st over the left. Break yarn and pull through the remaining st.

Sizing

Gauge
23 sts and 48 rows to 4 in. (10 cm) over garter st
Finished dimensions
4 in. (10 cm) tall x 4 in. (10 cm) wide triangle

Finishing

Lay the triangles flat and flip each pair to show the opposite side. Weave in all loose ends on the back. Block each piece to measurements. Thread a length of twine or string onto the tapestry needle and weave through the top of each triangle to make your garland, threading the triangles in any order you like.

Stripe pattern 1

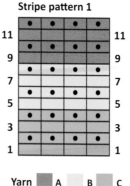

Yarn: A B C

Stripe pattern 2

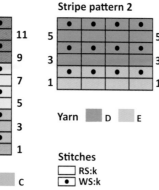

Yarn: D E

Stitches
RS:k
WS:k

Stripe pattern 3

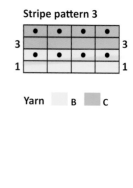

Yarn: B C

House Socks

Slip your feet into a cozy pair of chunky knit house socks. This pattern uses stripes with ribbing and cables for a twist on traditional stripes knit in plain stockinette. The stripes curve and dip with the cable twists, and blend into each other on the purl ribs. So much excitement in one technique!

Materials

- Cascade Yarns 128 Superwash, 100% superwash merino wool, 3.5 oz (100 g), 128 yds (117 m) 1 skein of each in the following shades:
  A; 1959, Deep Sapphire
  B; 1910, Summer Sky Heather

Needles and Notions

- Set of 5 US 10 (6 mm) double-pointed needles (DPNs)
- Length of similar thickness scrap yarn in a contrasting color
- Stitch marker
- Cable needle
- Tapestry needle

Pattern Notes

These socks are knit top down with an afterthought heel. Purl through the back loop for cleaner and tighter purl stitches. This is especially helpful for ribbing.
Carry the yarn on the inside of the sock up the beginning of the round, working two-row stripes of each color.

Sizing

Gauge
16 sts and 22 rows to 4 in. (10 cm) over St st

Finished dimensions
Womens Small/Medium to fit US 7-9, foot length 9¼ in. (23.5 cm).
Womens Large to fit US 9½-10, foot length 10¾ in. (27 cm)

Instructions (make 2)

With A, loosely cast on 40 sts. Divide sts evenly over 4 needles and join for working in the round taking care not to twist the sts and pm for beg of rnd.
Rnds 1 and 2: [k2, p2] rep to end.
Rnds 3 and 4: join B, [k2, p2] rep to end.
Rnds 5 and 6: using A, [k2, p2] rep to end.
Rnds 7 and 8: using B, k2, p2, k10, p2, [k2, p2] to end.

Rnds 9 and 10: using A, k2, p2, k10, p2, [k2, p2] to end.
Rnd 11: using B, k2, p2, slip next 5 sts purlwise to cable needle and hold at back of work, k5, k5 sts from cable needle, p2, [k2, p2] to end.
Rnd 12: k2, p2, k10, p2, [k2, p2] to end.
Rnds 13 & 14: rep Rnds 9 and 10.
Rep Rnds 7-14 twice more, then rep Rnds 7-12 only once more.
Break B and continue in A only to end.

Set-up afterthought heel: k2, p2, k10, p2, k2, with waste yarn k20. Using A, knit over the waste yarn sts continuing the original round.
Next rnd: k2, p2, k10, p2, k to end. Rep Rnds 7-14 another 4 times for size Small/Medium, and 5 times more for size Large.

Toe Decrease
Next rnd: Using A, ssk, k14, k2tog, k2, ssk, k14, k2tog, k2. (4 sts decreased)
Next rnd: knit.
Next rnd: ssk, k12, k2tog, k2, ssk, k12, k2tog, k2. (4 sts decreased)
Rep last round another 6 times, decreasing the k12 by 2 sts on each following rnd. (8 sts)
Break yarn leaving an 8 in. (20 cm) tail and use Kitchener stitch to close the toe.

Heel
Using 2 DPNs, pick up 20 sts directly above and 20 sts below the waste yarn sts.
With a third DPN, carefully pull out the waste yarn.
Divide the 20 sts above and 20 sts below the new heel opening onto 2 needles with 10 sts on each needle.
Join A to the bottom right-hand edge of the heel opening with the cuff closest to you, and the toe away from you. This DPN will be referred to as the first needle, with needles 2, 3, and 4 following it clockwise.

Rnd 1: k and AT THE SAME TIME pick up 2 sts on either side of the heel opening to prevent holes. The extra sts will be on the second and fourth DPNs. Redistribute the sts evenly so that each needle has 11 sts. Your new starting st will have moved 1 st to the right of the original.
Rnd 2: knit.
Rnd 3: k1, ssk, k to the last 3 sts of the second needle, k2tog, k1, ssk, k to the last 3 sts of the fourth needle, k2tog, k1. (4 sts decreased)
Rnd 4: knit.
Rnds 5 & 6: rep Rnds 3 and 4. (4 sts decreased)
Rep Rnd 3 only until 16 sts remain. Divide the top and bottom heel sts evenly over 2 DPNs (8 sts on each) and kitchener stitch the heel closed.

Finishing
Weave in all loose ends.
Block to finished dimensions.

Slip-Stitch Knitting

SLIP STITCHES CAN EASILY GIVE YOU THE SLIP BY TRICKING YOU INTO THINKING THEY'RE HARDER TO KNIT THAN THEY ACTUALLY ARE. IT ALMOST FEELS LIKE CHEATING BECAUSE DETAILED AND IMPRESSIVE COLOR PATTERNS CAN BE MADE WITH VERY LITTLE EFFORT. THE NUMBER OF SLIP STITCH COMBINATIONS ARE LIMITLESS, AND THE BEAUTY OF THIS SIMPLE TECHNIQUE IS THAT IT CAN LOOK INCREDIBLY DIFFERENT FROM PATTERN TO PATTERN.

A branch of the stripe technique, slip-stitch patterns also use just one color of yarn for the entire row. The difference between slip stitch and stripe patterns is that in slip stitch, while a color is worked across a row, stitches are also being slipped from the left-hand needle to the right-hand needle without being worked. This slipping technique creates seemingly elaborate stitch patterns by stretching out the height of the stitch, and elongating colors from the row below it. As stitches are stretched, they lose their elasticity, and can form a stiffer fabric, depending on the number of slip stitches used and the needle size. Smaller needles tend to form more rigid fabrics because the stitches are smaller and have less room to stretch. Larger needles can help to create more pliable fabrics because the larger stitches have more room to move.

Color Row Repeats

Colors in slip-stitch patterns are often worked in even numbers of rows in flat knitting, as they are for stripes. Doing this brings the working yarn back to the same beginning point where colors from each row can be loosely twisted up along one edge—leaving very little to weave in.

When working odd numbers of color rows in flat knitting, yarns can be carried up both sides of the work. Simply carry the yarn up the left side of the work when you come to it. Odd-numbered color row repeats are easily done when knitting in the round because the end of the "row" comes right back to the beginning, and the ends are readily available for twisting together.

Slipping Stitches

Stitches are always slipped purlwise and with the yarn held in the back of the work—with yarn in back (wyib), unless specifically stated to slip knitwise or with the yarn held in the front of the work—with yarn in front (wyif). Slipping wyif is usually done in flat knitting when working on the wrong side, or it can be used on both sides to create different effects. Slipping knitwise is not very common because it twists the stitch to sit opposite the rest of the stitches on the needle, but in some cases it is called for.

1

1 Slipping purlwise, or as if to purl, means that the right-hand needle is inserted into the back of the next stitch as if to purl. Instead of purling the stitch, it's lifted off the left-hand needle onto the right-hand needle. This places the stitch facing the same way as the rest of the stitches on the right-hand needle.

2 Slipping knitwise, or as if to knit, means that the right-hand needle is inserted into the front of the stitch as if to knit. Instead of knitting it, the stitch is lifted onto the right-hand needle and sits opposite the worked stitches.

2

Sample Slip-Stitch Patterns

Brick Pattern

Garter stitches are incorporated into a brick pattern to create texture and dimension, with the dark blue garter stitches moving forward, and the teal stockinette stitches receding. This pattern still retains elasticity because of the garter stitch rows.

Begin by casting on with A and knitting the first row.

Speckled Pattern

This speckled pattern shows slip stitches with the yarn held in front, and with the yarn held in back. The stitches slipped with the yarn held in front create what looks like dotted or dashed lines across the row. Stitches with the yarn held in back are slightly elongated.

Begin by casting on with A and purling the first row.

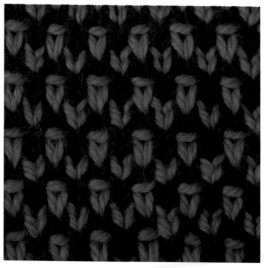

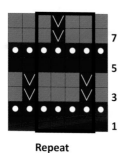

Brick mult. 4 + 3 sts

Yarn ■ A ■ B

Stitches
- ☐ RS: k, WS:p
- ● WS:k
- ⌄ RS: s1; WS: s1 wyif

Repeat

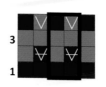

Speckle mult. of 2 + 3 sts

Yarn ■ A ■ B

Repeat

Stitches
- ☐ RS: k, WS:p
- ⌄ s1
- ⩔ s1 WS: s1 wyif

Zigzag Pattern

Bold, graphic lines can also be created with slip stitches—it's all in the placement. This zigzag pattern moves diagonally across the fabric, and has a completely different look and feel to the other slip stitch samples.

Begin by casting on with A and purling the first row.

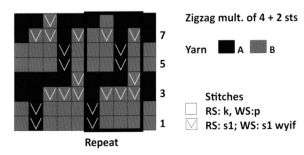

Repeat

Zigzag mult. of 4 + 2 sts

Yarn ■ A ■ B

Stitches
☐ RS: k, WS:p
☑ RS: s1; WS: s1 wyif

Materials

- Debbie Bliss Cashmerino Aran, 55% extrafine merino wool, 33% acrylic microfiber, 12% cashmere, 1.75 oz (50 g), 98 yds (90 m) 1 skein of each in the following shades:
  A; 300502, Pea Green
  B; 300004, Navy

Needles and Notions

- US 6 (4 mm) circular needles, 16 in. (40 cm) length
- US 8 (6 mm) circular needles, 16 in. (40 cm) length
- US 8 (6 mm) double-pointed needles (DPNs)
- 8 stitch markers
- Tapestry needle
- Pom-pom maker or cardboard for making pom-pom template

Bobble Hat

Speckled slip stitches adorn the crown of this unisex hat, which is topped off with a pom-pom. This hat looks like it could be a stranded colorwork pattern, but is actually made using slip stitches, working with only one yarn at a time. For a slouchier hat, knit in plain stockinette for a few more inches after the chart pattern.

Pattern Notes

All slip stitches are slipped purlwise.

Sizing

Gauge
20 sts and 24 rows to 4 in. (10 cm) over St st

Finished dimensions
One size; 21-23 in. (53.5-58 cm) head circumference, 9 in. (23 cm) tall excluding pom-pom

Chart Pattern

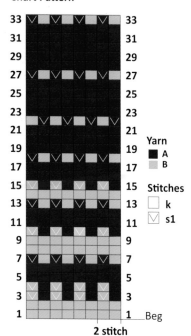

Yarn
■ A
■ B

Stitches
☐ k
⊻ s1

2 stitch repeat

Instructions

With A and US 6 (4 mm) circular needle, cast on 104 sts, join for working in the round taking care not to twist the sts and pm for beg of rnd.
Work k1, p1 rib for 1 in. (2.5 cm).

Change to US 8 (6 mm) circular needles.
Join in B at row 3 and work through all rows of the chart.
Using A yarn only, work in St st (knit every round) until piece measures 6 in. (15 cm) from the cast-on edge.

Decrease crown

Next rnd: [k13, pm] to end.
Decrease rnd: [k to 2 sts before marker, k2tog] to end. (8 sts decreased)
Next rnd: knit.
Rep last 2 rnds another 6 times. (48 sts)
Rep Decrease rnd only until 8 sts

remain, changing to DPNs when stitches are not comfortably held on circular needles anymore.
Break yarn leaving a 6 in. (15 cm) tail and use the tapestry needle to weave the end through the remaining stitches and secure.

Finishing

Weave in all loose ends.
Block hat to finished dimensions.

Using A and a pom-pom maker or template cut from card, make a 2 in. (5 cm) pom-pom. Leave a long tail when tying the pom-pom for attaching to the top of the hat. Securely stitch the pom-pom in place.

Pocketed Scarf

Keep your hands warm, tuck away small treasures, and look great while wrapped up in this cozy scarf; it's sure to be a winter favorite! Knit in one very long piece, with the slip stitch pattern worked on the pockets only. The right side changes to the opposite side for the body of the scarf, so when the pockets are folded up, the patterns will line up correctly. The two colors for each chart are carried up the side of the piece for that section. This is a very chunky knit with the yarn held double throughout giving it a nice weight and warmth.

Materials

- Brown Sheep Lamb's Pride Worsted, 85% wool, 15% mohair, 4 oz (113 g), 190 yds (173 m)
  3 skeins of A; shade M-05, Onyx
  1 skein of each in the following shades:
  C; M-155 Lemon Drop
  D; M-38, Lotus Pink
- Brown Sheep Lanaloft Worsted Weight 100% wool, 3.5 oz. (100 g), 160 yds. (146 m)
  1 skein of (B) shade LL27W, Sea Fog

Needles and Notions

- US 11 (8 mm) knitting needles
- Tapestry needle

Pattern Notes

All slip stitches are slipped purlwise.

Instructions

With A held double, cast on 25 sts. Knit 4 rows in garter stitch.

Pocket section
With all yarns held double throughout, follow the Pocket Chart, joining B, and carrying yarns A and B up the side for rows 1-12.
Join C at row 13 and work rows 15-22 6 times in total carrying C and D up along the right hand side.
Join A and rep Rows 11 and 12 once.
Join B and rep Rows 1-10, carrying yarns A and B up the side once.
Join A and knit 4 rows in garter stitch.

Body of scarf
Next row (new WS): k3, p to last 3 sts, k3.
Next row (new RS): knit.
Rep last 2 rows until piece measures 60 in. (152.5 cm) from cast-on edge ending with a RS row.
Knit 4 rows in garter stitch.
Rep Pocket Section once more.
Bind off all sts.

Finishing
Block piece to 76 x 8 in. (193 cm x 20.5 cm).
Fold the ends up 8 in. (20.5 cm) with the WS of the pockets together, and stitch the sides together.
Weave in all loose ends.

Sizing

Gauge
12 sts and 16 rows to 4 in. (10 cm) over St st with yarn held double

Finished dimensions
60 x 8 in. (152.5 x 20.5 cm)

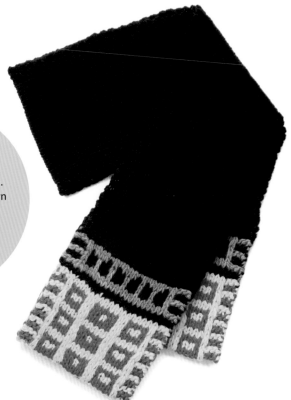

Pocket Chart

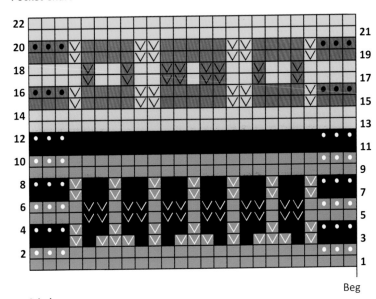

Beg

Stitches
- ☐ RS: k, WS:p
- ⦿ WS: k
- ⋁ RS: s1; WS: s1 wyif

Yarn
- ■ A
- ■ B
- ☐ C
- ■ D

Leg Warmers

A fun, simple slip stitch pattern for leg warmers incorporating garter stitch into the design, which adds stretch. The honeycomb shapes may look difficult, but that's only a trick of the technique. If you like slouchy leg warmers add extra repeats for more length. The bottom edge fans out a bit, making them a nice slip over for boots or heels.

Materials

- Cascade 220, 100% wool, 3.5 oz (100 g), 220 yds (200 m) 1 skein each of the following shades:
  A; 9459, Yakima Heather
  B; 2433, Pacific

Needles and Notions

- US 5 (3.75 mm) double-pointed needles (DPNs)
- US 7 (4.5 mm) double-pointed needles (DPNs)
- Tapestry needle

Sizing

Gauge
21 sts and 28 rows = 4 in. (10 cm) in honeycomb pattern

Finished dimensions
Upper calf circumference, Small (Medium,Large):
12 (13¾, 16¾)in./30.5 (35, 42.5)cm
Length S (M,L): 14 (15, 16)in. /35.5 (38, 40.5)cm

Pattern Notes

All slip stitches are slipped purlwise.
Carry yarns up the inside at the beginning of the round.

Honeycomb Chart

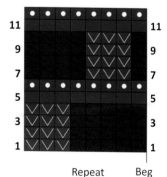

Repeat   Beg

Stitches
- ☐ k
- ⦿ p
- ▽ sl

Yarn
- ■ A
- ■ B

Instructions (make 2)

With A and size 5 (3.75 mm) DPNs, cast on 64 (72, 88) sts. Divide sts evenly over the needles and join for working in the round taking care not to twist the sts. Use the cast-on tail to mark the beginning of the round.

Rnds 1-7: [k2, p2] rep to end.
Rnd 8: knit.
Change to size 7 (4.5 mm) DPNs.
Rnd 9: join B and knit.
Rnd 10: purl.
Rnds 11-12: rep Rows 9 and 10.

Commence Honeycomb Chart:
Rnds 1-4: join A, [k5, sl3] rep to end.
Rnd 5: join B, knit.
Rnd 6: purl.
Rnds 7-10: join A, k1, [sl3, k5] rep to last 7 sts, sl3, k4.
Rnds 11-12: rep Rows 17 and 18.

Size Small only: rep Rnds 1-12 another 6 times.
Size Medium only: rep Rnds 1-12 another 6 times then rows 1-6 once more.
Size Large only: rep Rnds 1-12 another 7 times.

Break A and continue in B only.
Next rnd: knit.
Next rnd: purl.
Rep these 2 rnds another 4 times.

Finishing

Bind off. Weave in all loose ends and block to finished dimensions.
The bottom will fan out a little bit and the top will pull in and hug the calf.

Materials

- Brown Sheep Lanaloft Worsted, 100% wool, 3.5 oz. (100 g), 160 yds (146 m) 3 skeins of A; LL36W, Dark Ash
  2 skeins of B; LL57W, Lemon Pound Cake
  1 skein of C; LL33W, Manor Gray

Needles and Notions

- US 7 (4.5 mm) circular needle: 36 in. (90 cm) length for 38-42 in. (96.5-106.5 cm) chest, 40 in. (100 cm) length for 46-50 in. (117-127 cm) chest, and 47 in. (120 cm) length for 54 in. (137 cm) chest
- US 9 (5.5 mm) circular needle: 36 in. (90 cm) length for 38-42 in. (96.5-106.5 cm) chest, 40 in. (100 cm) length for 46-50 in. (117-127 cm) chest, and 47 in. (120 cm) length for 54 in. (137 cm) chest
- US 7 (4.5 mm) circular needle, 20 in. (50 cm) length
- US 9 (5.5 mm) circular needle, 20 in. (50 cm) length
- Stitch marker
- Stitch holder or scrap yarn
- Tapestry needle

Man's Vest

Knit a simple checkerboard pattern using slip stitches to create what appears to be a complicated colorwork piece. This vest uses two shades of gray with a pop of yellow for a fun look on any occasion! Pair it with jeans and an unbuttoned collar, or dress it up with a suit and tie.

The vest is knit from the bottom upward in the round until the armholes, the yoke is then worked flat in rows. When knitting flat, remember to slip stitches with yarn in front on the wrong side, keeping all the slip stitches uniform.

Sizing

Gauge

20 sts and 20 rows to 4 in. (10 cm) over check pattern

Finished dimensions

Mens chest size: 38 (42, 46, 50, 54) in. / 96.5 (106.5, 117, 127, 137) cm

Pattern Notes

All slip stitches are slipped purlwise.

CHECKERBOARD PATTERN (worked in the round)
Rnd 1: join B, knit.
Rnds 2-3: join C, [k2, sl2 wyib] rep to end.
Rnd 4: rep Row 1.
Rnds 5-6: join A, [sl2 wyib, k2] rep to end.

CHECKERBOARD PATTERN (worked flat in rows)
Row 1 (RS): join B, knit
Row 2 (WS): join C, [sl2 wyif, p2] rep to end.
Row 3: [k2, sl2 wyib] rep to end.
Row 4: join B, purl.
Row 5: join A, [sl2 wyib, k2] rep to end.
Row 6: [p2, sl2 wyif] rep to end.

Checkerboard Chart

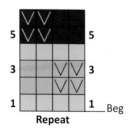

Repeat

Beg

Yarn
- A
- B
- C

Stitches
- RS: k, WS:p
- RS:s1; WS:s1 wyif

Instructions

With US 7 (4.5 mm), 36 in. (90 cm) circular needles and A, cast on 188 (212, 232, 252, 272) sts, pm and join for working in the round taking care not to twist the sts.
Work [K3, p1] rib for 3 in. (7.5 cm).

Change to US 9 (5.5 mm), 36 in. (90 cm) needles and work the checkerboard pattern until piece measures 13 (14, 14½, 15, 16) in. / 33 (35.5, 37, 38, 40.5) cm, or desired length from cast-on edge.

For the yoke, divide stitches equally placing 94 (106, 116, 126, 136) sts on a stitch holder.

Back

Work the checkerboard pattern flat in rows as set, keeping the pattern straight as you work the shaping:

**Bind off 5 (5, 5, 6, 7) sts at beginning of next 2 rows; 84 (96, 106, 114, 122) sts.
Bind off 3 sts at beginning of next 2 rows; 78 (90, 100, 108, 116) sts.
Decrease 1 st at each end on every RS row 4 (5, 6, 8, 9) times; 70 (80, 88, 92, 98) sts **.

Continue straight in checkerboard pattern until armholes measure 9½ (9¾, 11, 12, 13) in. / 24 (25, 28, 30.5, 33) cm.

Shape shoulders

Bind off 7 (8, 9, 9, 9) sts at beginning of next 2 rows.
Bind off 6 (8, 8, 8, 9) sts at beginning of next 2 rows.
Bind off 6 (7, 8, 8, 9) sts at beginning of next 2 rows.
Bind off remaining 32 (34, 38, 42, 44) sts.

Front

Slip held sts to working needle and work as for Back from ** to **.
Continue straight in checkerboard pattern until armholes measure 3 (3, 4½, 4¾, 5) in. / 7.5 (7.5, 11.5, 12, 12.5) cm from first armhole bind off row.

Next RS row: Work 35 (40, 44, 46, 49) sts to center of row, turn and work left shoulder as follows, leaving remaining sts on hold.

Continue working armhole shaping, and at the same time dec. 1 st at neck edge every RS edge 12 (13, 16, 18, 19) times.

Decrease 1 st at neck edge every 4 rows, 4 (4, 3, 3, 3) times; 19 (23, 25, 25, 27) sts.

Work straight in checkerboard pattern until armhole matches the Back, and shape shoulders as for the Back.
Repeat for the opposite side of neck, reversing neck and shoulder shaping.

Finishing

Block pieces to finished measurements.
Sew the shoulder seams.

Neck and armhole ribbing

With US 7 (4.5 mm), 20 in. (50 cm) circular needles and A, pick up and knit approximately 3 sts for every 4 rows at each armhole. Join for working in the round taking care not to twist the sts and pm for beg of rnd; 72 (72, 80, 88, 96) sts.

Work 3x1 rib pattern for ¾ in. (2 cm). Bind off in rib. Weave in all loose ends.

For V-neck edging, starting at the Front center, pick up sts as for armhole; 72 (76, 80, 88, 92) sts.

Work 1 round in 3x1 rib and then decrease at center Front every other row as follows: sl2tog kwise, k1, psso. Bind off in pattern and weave in all loose ends.

Measurements

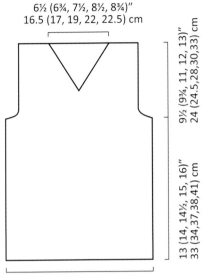

6½ (6¾, 7½, 8½, 8¾)"
16.5 (17, 19, 22, 22.5) cm

9½ (9¾, 11, 12, 13)"
24 (24.5,28,30,33) cm

13 (14, 14½, 15, 16)"
33 (34,37,38,41) cm

Chest circumference
38 (42, 46, 50, 54)"
97 (107, 117, 127, 137) cm

Chevron Rug

Add a small chevron rug to any little nook of your home—it might lay by the nightstand, dresser, or even the bathroom sink. The bold geometric pattern makes a wonderful statement piece with bright, contrasting colors, or a subtle one with muted, monochromatic hues. Either way, it's a quick chunky knit with a seed stitch border.

Materials

- Patons Classic Wool Roving, 100 % wool, 3.5 oz (100 g), 120 yds (109 m) 2 skeins of each in the following shades:
  A; 77306, Plum
  B; 77605, Pumpkin
  C; 77203, Pacific Teal

Needles and Notions

- US 13 (9 mm) knitting needles
- Tapestry needle

Yarn

■ A ■ B ▨ C

Stitches

☐ RS: k, WS:p
∨ RS:s1; WS:s1 wyif

Pattern Notes

Yarn is not carried up between color changes. Break the yarn after each color section and weave in ends.
All slip stitches are slipped purlwise.

Chevron Chart

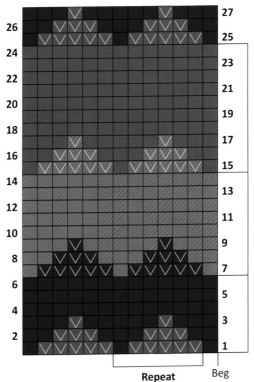

Repeat   Beg

10 Row Section

8 Row Section

6 Row Section

Sizing

Gauge
10 sts and 12 rows to 4 in. (10 cm) over St st with yarn held double

Finished dimensions
18 x 28 in. (46 x 71 cm)

Instructions

With A held double, cast on 43 sts.
Rows 1-4: [k1, p1] to last st, k1.
Row 5 (WS): k1, p1, k1, p to last 3 sts, k1, p1, k1.
Row 6 (RS): k1, p1, k2, [sl5, k1] to last 3 sts, k1, p1, k1.
Row 7: k1, p1, k1, p2, [sl3, p3] to last 8 sts, sl3, p2, k1, p1, k1.
Row 8: k1, p1, k1, k3, [sl1, k5] to last 7 sts, sl1, k3, k1, p1, k1.
Row 9: k1, p1, k1, p to last 3 sts, k1, p1, k1.
Row 10: k1, p1, k1, k to last 3 sts, k1, p1, k1.
Row 11: rep Row 9.

Color Sections

6-Row Section; Rep Rows 6-8 once more, rep Rows 9 and 10 once then row 9 only once more.
8 Row Section; Rep Rows 6-8 once more, rep Rows 9 and 10 twice, then row 9 only once more.
10 Row Section; Rep Rows 6-8 once more, rep Rows 9 and 10 3 times, then row 9 only once more.

Continue to work with the yarn held double throughout, changing colors as given in the sequence below:
With B work 10-row section.
With C work 6-row section.
With A work 8-row section.
With B work 6-row section.

With C work 10-row section.
With A work 6-row section.
With B work 8-row section.
With C work 6-row section.
With A work 10-row section.
With B work 6-row section.
With C work 8-row section.
With A work 6-row section.

Continue with A only as follows:
Next 4 rows: [k1, p1] to last st, k1.
Bind off sts.

Finishing

Weave in all loose ends.
Block to finished dimensions.

Materials

- Brown Sheep Lamb's Pride Worsted, 85% wool, 15% mohair, 4 oz (113 g), 190 yds (173 m) 1 skein of A; shade M38, Lotus Pink
- Valley Yarns Berkshire, 85% wool, 15% alpaca, 3.5 oz (100g), 141 yds (129 m) 1 skein of each in the following shades:
B; 44, Tan Heather
C; 12, Orange

Needles and Notions

- US 9 (5.5 mm) knitting needles
- US 7 (4.5 mm) double-pointed needles (DPNs)
- 50 in. (127 cm) cord for strap
- Tapestry needle

Purse

Three colors are used to create this textured slip stitch purse. It incorporates slipping with the yarn held in front and in back, and shows how the different colors lay over each other. The resulting linen stitch produces a tight, flat fabric, which works well for a purse as it prevents things from poking out between the stitches. It almost feels like a reversible fabric, but you'll notice that the reverse side does look slightly different than the front.

Sizing

Gauge:
18 sts and 15 rows to 4 in. (10 cm) over linen st on US 9 (5.5 mm) needles

Finished dimensions:
5½ x 7½ in. (14 x 19 cm)

Pattern Notes

All slip stitches are slipped purlwise.
Carry the unused yarns up the side.

Linen stitch

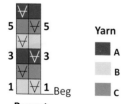

Yarn
■ A
□ B
■ C

Repeat

Stitches
☐ RS: k; WS:p
☒ RS:s1 wyif; WS:s1

Instructions

With US 9 (5.5 mm) needles and A, cast on 27 sts.
Rows 1-4: knit.
Row 5: join B, k1, [sl1 wyif, k1] rep to end.
Row 6: join C, p2, [sl1 wyib, p1] rep to last st, p1.
Row 7: join A, rep Row 5.
Row 8: join B, rep Row 6.
Row 9: join C, rep Row 5.
Row 10: join A, rep Row 6.

Rep Rows 5-10 until piece measures 15 in. (38 cm) from cast-on edge.
Next 4 rows: using A, knit 4 rows.
Bind off sts. Weave in all loose ends.

Strap
With DPNs and A, cast on 4 sts. Work 45 in. (114 cm) of I-cord (see page 19).
Thread the store-bought cord through the center of the I-cord to prevent stretching. See page 19 more for help.

Finishing
Block the purse to 6 x 16 in. (15 x 41 cm).
Fold in half lengthways and Kitchener stitch the sides together. Secure cord inside the I-cord, and stitch the straps to the inside sides of the purse.

Intarsia Knitting

ADD A BOLD GRAPHIC IMAGE OR A COLORFUL GEOMETRIC PATTERN TO ANY KNITTED PIECE WITH INTARSIA, A TECHNIQUE WHICH KNITS BOLD, COLORFUL DESIGNS INTO THE FABRIC.

Intarsia knitting lets you join one or more colors of yarn together to create a colorful fabric. It's great for knitting a picture or graphic image, or making larger color blocks throughout a design. Intarsia differs from stranded knitting in that it uses separate yarns for each color section rather than floating the yarn across the back. The color changes in intarsia are twisted together to prevent holes. Stranded knitting tends to be stiffer and thicker than intarsia knitting, which creates a knitted fabric that drapes and moves like a plain stockinette.

Intarsia may look intimidating, but you can start off with just two colors, and work up to a design with twelve different colors. Either way, the motions are still the same—it's just the number of yarns that you have to manage. With a little practice intarsia can be a breeze—it's all the yarn ends that'll take some time to weave in!

Tips

- Intarsia is generally worked in stockinette and flat rows because it's easier to knit the color sections back and forth.
- Weave in ends as you go.
- Use a ruler above each chart row to help you remember where you are in the pattern.

Step-by-step

Preparing the Yarn: Bobbins and Butterflies

To begin a project, you'll need to prepare all the different colored yarns you need. Wind 2–4 yds (2–3.5 m) of yarn onto a small bobbin, or into yarn butterflies. You will unwind enough to knit each section without the yarns becoming tangled. Don't worry too much about the amount of yarn wound for each section you—can join in more if you run out. To make a yarn butterfly, wind yarn in a figure "8" between your thumb and forefinger. Stop about 5 in. (12.5 cm) from the end of your yarn and wrap the tail around the middle of the butterfly and make a slipknot to secure. Pull yarn from the other end to knit with.

Joining a New Color

1 Place the yarn between the needles, leaving a 6 in. (15 cm) tail at the front of your work, and your yarn supply in the back. Leaving the tail at the front helps to hold the tail in place and makes it less confusing as to which end to knit with.

1

2 Drop the old color and wrap the new yarn under and to the right of the old yarn, twisting the old and new yarns together. Knit as usual.

Join a new color on the back of the work in the same way as the front. Leave a 6 in. (15 cm) tail at the front, and drop the old color. Wrap the new color under and to the right of the old yarn, and purl as usual. Follow pattern to join and change colors, then weave in all ends.

2

Designing Your Own Intarsia Charts

Creating your own designs is a great way to personalize any project. If you're adding a motif to an existing pattern, such as a sweater or hat, count the number of stitches and rows available before you begin to design your image. Adding a motif to a section of plain stockinette is the best way to start as it's a blank canvas and won't be interrupted by stitch patterns.

When designing intarsia patterns, keep in mind that stockinette stitches are not square. So, do not use regular graph paper: Find or make your own graph paper with a rectangular grid so your chart will be proportional to your knitting, or photocopy the knitting grid on page 141. Alternatively you can use a word processor to make your own grids. Use colored pencils or markers to draw the design onto the paper. If you find yourself designing a lot of patterns you may want to buy specialist knitting chart software. This will allow you to add and change colors easily, which can make the design process more efficient.

Below and on the next few pages are a few samples of intarsia designs for inspiration.

Knapsack,
see page 84

Panda Chart

This pattern just uses two colors to form a sweet panda face.

Yarn A ■ B

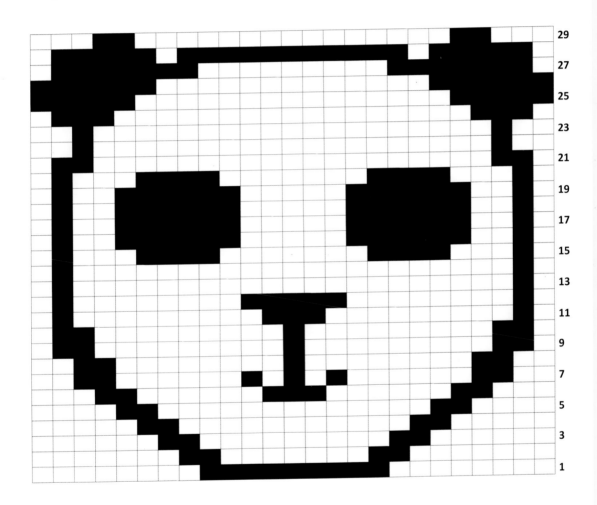

Stitches
☐ RS: k, WS:p

Cupcake Chart

Using just one section of color at time, the yarns in this cupcake pattern are very easy to manage.

Yarn A B C D E

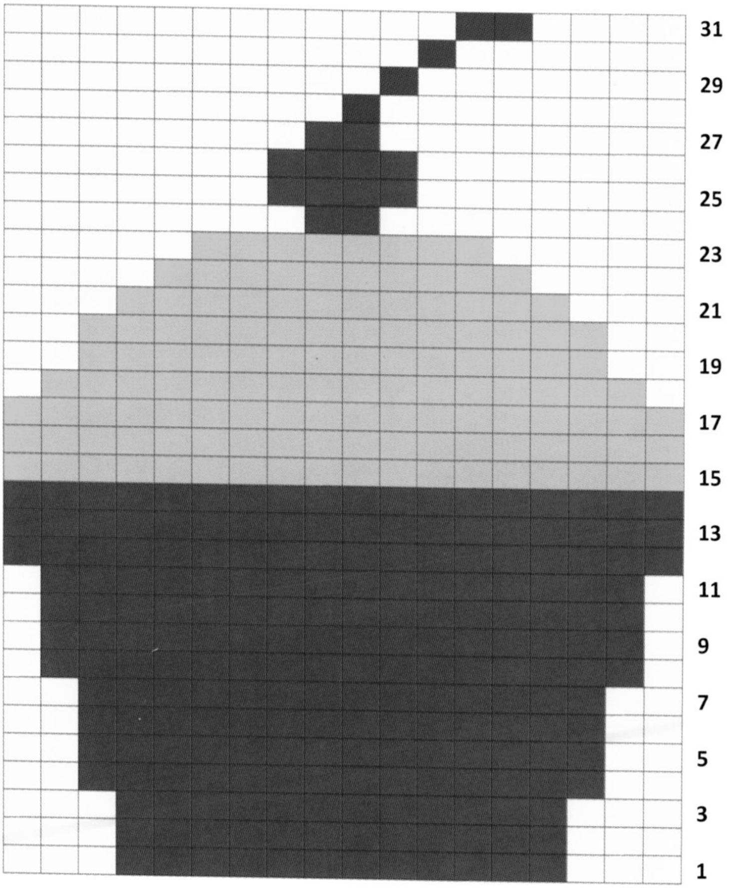

Stitches

☐ **RS: k, WS:p**

Squares Chart

Intarsia patterns can be used as an allover pattern—not just for one section. These simple blocks of color can be used to make a multicolored fabric such as a blanket, scarf, or even a sweater.

Yarn  A B C D

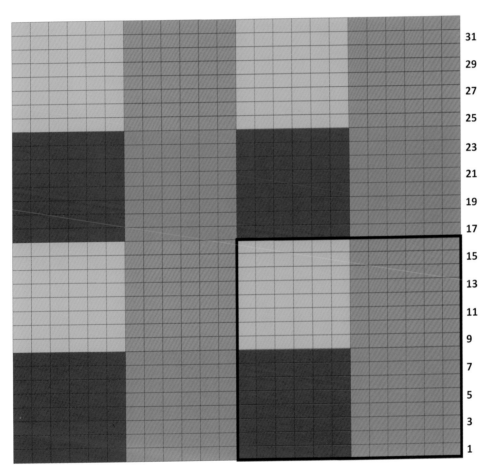

Repeat

Stitches
☐ RS: k, WS:p

Materials

- Debbie Bliss Cotton DK, 100% cotton, 50 g (1.75 oz), 92 yds (84 m) 1 ball of each in the following shade:
- A; 13039, teal
- B; 13064, coral

Needles and Notions

- US 6 (4 mm) knitting needles
- G (4mm) crochet hook
- Yarn bobbin (optional)
- Stitch markers
- Tapestry needle
- ⅜ in. (1 cm) button
- Sewing needle and thread to match yarn A

Pattern Notes

You can carry color B across the back of the stitches at the center of the heart chart—in Rows 8 and 9—so you don't have to attach new yarn for the few chart stitches that are left.

Heart Chart

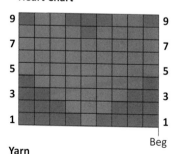

Beg

Yarn

◼ A ◼ B

Stitches

☐ RS: k, WS:p

Detachable Collar

This cute project is sure to pull at the heart strings. A sweet and simple collar that's a great first intarsia project, with just one color change and motif. It's a lovely addition to blouses or dresses and will brighten up any outfit!

Instructions

Using A, cast on 110 sts.
Rows 1 and 3: [k1, p1] rep to end.
Row 2: [p1, k1] rep to end.
Row 4: p1, k1, p1, p to last 3 sts, k1, p1, k1.
Row 5: k1, p1, k2, work row 1 of Heart Chart, k8, ssk, pm, k2tog, [k18, ssk, pm, k2tog] 3 times, k8, work row 1 of Heart Chart, k1, p1.
Continue working through the Heart Chart on either end of the collar as set for the next 8 rows.
Rows 6, 8, 10, 12, 14: p1, k1, p1, p to last 3 sts, k1, p1, k1.
Rows 7, 9, 11, 13, 15: k1, p1, k1, [k to 2 sts before marker, ssk, sm, k2tog] 4 times, k to last 3 sts, p1, k1, p1. (8 sts decreased per row)
Rows 16 and 18: [p1, k1] rep to end.
Row 17: [k1, p1] rep to end.
Bind off sts but do not fasten off last st.

Slip st to crochet hook, ch 16 and, using the tapestry needle, secure end to make a fastening loop at the right-hand corner.

Finishing

With a sewing needle and thread held quadruple, sew the button to the top-left corner of the collar. Weave in all loose ends, weaving the heart ends along the outer edge of the back of the heart.
Block to finished dimensions.

Sizing

Gauge
20 sts and 26 rows to 4 in. (10 cm) over St st
Finished dimensions
14 in. (35.5 cm) top collar edge, 22 in. (57 cm) bottom collar edge, 3 in. (7.5 cm) tall

Materials

- Patons Classic Wool Merino, 100% wool, 223 yds, (204 m), 3.5 oz, (100 g) 2 skeins of A; 187379, Winter White
- Brown Sheep Co. Nature Spun Worsted, 100% wool, 3.5 oz (100 g), 245 yds (224 m) 1 skein of each in the following shades:
  B; 305, Impasse Yellow
  E; N17, French Clay
  F; N46, Red Fox
  G; N85, Peruvian Pink
  I; 205, Regal Purple
  K; N78, Turquoise Wonder
  L; N24, Evergreen
  M; 131, Lemon Grass
- Brown Sheep Co. Lamb's Pride Superwash Worsted, 100% wool, 3.5 oz, (100 g), 200 yds (183 m) 1 skein of C; SW193, Wild Honey
- Blue Sky Alpacas, 100% cotton, 3.5 oz, (100 g), 150 yds (137 m) 1 skein each in the following shades:
  D; 601, Poppy
  H; 640, Hyacinth
  J; 632, Mediterranean

Needles and Notions

- US 6 (4 mm) knitting needles
- Scissors
- Tapestry needle
- 12 in. (30.5 cm) pillow pad

Color Wheel Cushion

A bright color wheel pillow is perfect inspiration for your colorwork projects and is sure to liven up any room! This pillow is knit in two square panels then stitched together. It uses all twelve colors from the color wheel, so it's a great practice piece for intarsia knitting and interlocking yarns together.

Color Wheel Chart

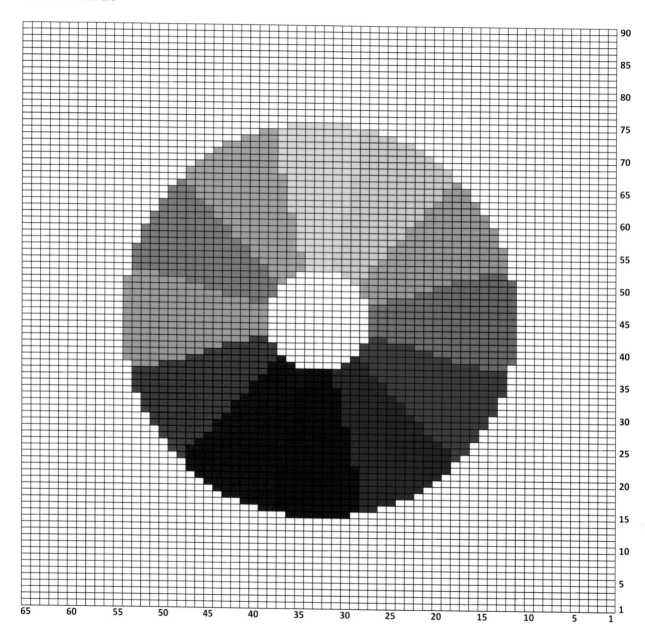

Pattern Notes

To help your knitting move faster, make yarn butterflies or bobbins for all the colors before you begin.

Instructions

Front

With A, cast on 65 sts.
Beginning with a RS knit row, work in St st following the Color Wheel Chart and key for the color changes.
When the chart is complete, bind off all sts.

Back

With A, cast on 65 sts.
Beginning with a RS knit row, work in St st for 90 rows.
Bind off all sts leaving a long tail for sewing together.

Finishing

Weave in all loose ends and block both squares to 12" (30.5 cm) square.
Place wrong sides together (with right sides facing out) and Kitchener stitch around 3 sides. Insert the pillow cushion and continue stitching to close the case.

Yarn

- A Winter white
- B Impasse Yellow
- C Wild Honey
- D Poppy
- E French Clay
- F Red Fox
- G Peruvian Pink
- H Hyacinth
- I Regal Purple
- J Mediterranean
- K Turquoise Wonder
- L Ever Green
- M Lemon Grass

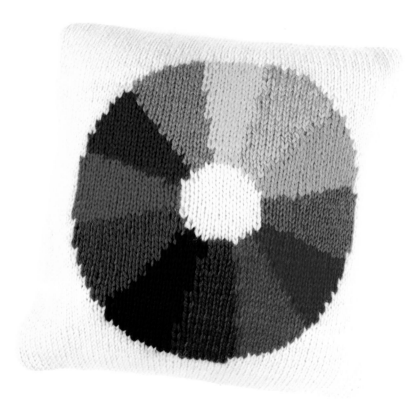

World Map Artwork

A unique world map to hang on your wall! This intarsia knit artwork is a great piece for any home. You can even customize it to your hometown by using duplicate stitch to add a red "dot" or stitch for your location. The stitch also kind of looks like a heart shape, which is a nice touch!

Materials

- Cascade 220 Superwash Sport, 100% superwash merino wool, 50 g (1.75 oz), 136 yds (125 m)
  1 skein of each in the following shades:
  A; 849, Dark Aqua
  B; 802 Green Apple

Needles and Notions

- US 6 (4 mm) knitting needles
- Bobbins for yarn (optional)
- Tapestry needle
- Matboard 8 x 11 in. (20 x 28 cm)
- Scissors
- Spray glue
- Picture frame 11 x 14 in. (28 x 35.5 cm)

Pattern Notes

When joining new fresh yarn to an existing yarn butterfly or bobbin, do so at the edge of a continent, or at the beginning or end of a row. This will help keep the map looking flat and smooth.

To join yarn on a wrong side row, leave a 6 in. (15 cm) tail hanging on the right side of the work, and the yarn bobbin hanging on the wrong side. With so many strands, this will help prevent you from knitting with the wrong yarn tail. You can move the tails to the wrong side once finished.

Resist the urge to strand yarn across more than one stitch in some places. Trust me, you'll be glad you didn't in the end. The map will look smoother and have less puckering.

World Map Chart

Yarn A B Stitches ☐ RS: k, WS:p

Tip

- Use duplicate stitch to work the smaller island countries once you have finished knitting the map.

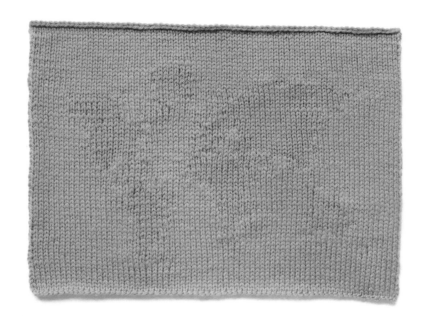

Sizing

Gauge

22 sts over 30 rows to 4 in. (10 cm) over St st

Finished dimensions

9½ x 13 in. (24 cm x 33 cm)

Instructions

Prepare yarn butterflies or bobbins of yarn B. You can start off with a few, and then make more as you go.

With A, cast on 72 sts. Row 1 will be the right side of your work. Follow the World Map Chart working from the bottom upward. Work to the end of row 72 and bind off all sts.

Finishing

Weave in all loose ends along the continent edges or beginning or ends of rows, on the wrong side of the work.

Use duplicate stitch to stitch in the smaller island countries that you skipped. Weaving in these ends gets a little tricky because they're so small, so just weave them up a couple of stitches, then back down. They don't need to be long weaves because the map will be mounted in

one place, as opposed to moving around constantly in a garment. Do the best you can to keep the yarn tails close to the island.

Block the map to the finished dimensions.

This map is made to fit a standard 8 x 11 in. (20 cm x 28 cm) matboard, and then into an 11 x 14 in. (28 x 35.5 cm) picture frame. There is extra "water" around the piece so it won't have to stretch to fit into the matboard. To help stabilize the map and make it easier to frame, cut a 9½ x 13 in. (24 cm x 33 cm) piece of matboard and spray with glue. Carefully mount your knitted map to the matboard, beginning at the bottom edge, and stretching it up evenly over the matboard. Wait a few minutes for the glue to dry, insert it into your frame, and enjoy it on your wall!

Ear Warmer

With its bold geometric pattern, this ear warmer band will keep you both cozy and stylish. The color pattern uses intarsia as an all-over pattern, making up the bulk of the piece. It's also knit tightly to help keep the cold and wind from seeping through to your ears.

Materials

- Brown Sheep Nature Spun Worsted, 100 % wool, 3.5 oz (100 g), 245 yds (224 m)
  1 skein of each in the following shades:
  A; 601W, Pepper
  B; 112, Elf Green
  C; 145, Salmon
  D; N87, Victorian Pink
  E; N91, Aran
- F; 305, Impasse Yellow

Needles and Notions

- US 9 (5.5 mm) knitting needles
- Tapestry needle
- Yarn bobbins (optional)

Sizing

Gauge
16 sts and 20 rows to 4 in. (10 cm) over St st with yarn held double

Finished dimensions
One size; 4 x 21 in. (10 x 53.5 cm)

Instructions

With A held double, cast on 82 sts.

Rows 1 and 2: knit.
Rows 3 and 4: join B, knit.
Rows 5-16: starting with a RS knit row, work in St st following the twenty-stitch repeat Geometric Chart 4 times across, and work the first 2 sts of the repeat for the last 2 sts of the row. This is to give room for sewing a seamless piece at the end.

Rows 17 and 18: join B, knit.
Rows 19 and 20: join A, knit.
Bind off all sts and break yarn leaving a long tail for sewing up.

Finishing
Block piece to 4 x 21 in. (10 x 53.5 cm). With a tapestry needle, Kitchener stitch the ends together to form the ear warmer.

Pattern Notes

Yarn is held double throughout. Make yarn butterflies or bobbins of all colors before beginning, to help your knitting move faster and remember to make the bobbins with the yarn held double.

Geometric Chart

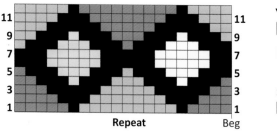

Repeat   Beg

Yarn

■ A   ▨ C

▨ D   ▨ E   ▨ F

Stitches
☐ RS: k, WS:p

Knapsack

This nature-inspired knapsack features three intarsia feathers. The body is knit in one piece and folded and stitched over two side panels, leaving a top flap with button closures. It's great for kids or adults on a day out.

Materials

- Brown Sheep Shepherd's Shades, 100% wool, 3.5 oz (100 g), 131 yds (118 m) 2 skeins of A; SS411, Maize
  1 skein of each in the following shades:
  B; SS791, Weathered Teal
  C; SS110, Pearl
  D; SS111 Chestnut

Needles and Notions

- US 10 (6 mm) knitting needles
- 2 buttons to match color D, 1½ in. (4 cm) diameter
- Tapestry needle
- Straight pins

Feather Chart

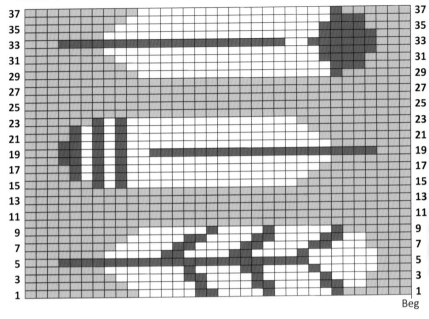

Yarn ☐ A ☐ B ■ C   Stitches ☐ RS: k, WS: p

Sizing

Gauge
16 sts and 24 rows to 4 in.
(10 cm) over St st
16 sts and 32 rows to 4 in.
(10 cm) over garter st

Finished dimensions
11 x 11½ x 2 in.
(28 x 29 x 5 cm)

Instructions

Body
With A, cast on 40 sts.
Rows 1-4: k in garter st.
Row 5 (RS): knit.
Row 6 (WS): k3, p to last 3 sts, k3.
Rep Rows 5 and 6 twice more.
Row 11 (bottom buttonhole row):
k6, bind off 4 sts, k to last 10 sts, bind off 4 sts, k6.
Row 12 (top buttonhole row): k3, p3, cable cast on 4 sts, and bring yarn to front before slipping last cast on st onto needle, p to beginning of the bind off, cable cast on 4 sts, p3, k3.
Rep Rows 5 and 6 another 45 times.

Begin following the Feather Chart and continue working the 3 st garter border at both ends throughout.
Next row (WS): k3, p to last 3 sts, k3.
Rep Rows 5 and 6 another 10 times.
Knit the next 4 rows in garter st.
Bind off all sts.

Side Panels
With A, CO 8 sts and knit in garter st until piece measures 10 ½ in.
Next row: k2tog, k to last 2 sts, ssk.
(2 sts decreased)
Next row: knit.
Repeat last 2 rows twice more and bind off last 2 sts.
Make another matching side panel.

Straps
With D, cast on 6 sts and knit 118 rows in garter st.
Bind off all sts, leaving a long tail for sewing up.
Make a second matching strap.

Finishing
Block the main body to 11 x 29 in. (28 x 74 cm), and 2 side panels to 11½ x 2 in. (29 x 5 cm).
Line up and pin the side panels with the garter st border on the main body, beginning at the bind off edge and working all around each side panel. Make sure both sides are even, and stitch together using a running stitch. There should be about 4 in. (10 cm) between the top flap and opening of the knapsack. Fold the flap down, making sure it doesn't cover the top feather, and mark where the buttons should go. Stitch them in place with B. Stitch the straps in place right next to the garter st border at the top and bottom of the back of the knapsack. Weave in all loose ends.

You can reinforce the knapsack by adding a fabric lining to the inside of the main bag and inside the straps.

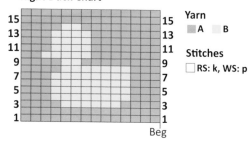

Baby Mitts

Sweet little yellow ducks adorn these tiny newborn mittens. They're worked flat and seamed on one side to make it easier to knit the intarsia pattern. There are two charts for the ducks—one for each hand so they're facing each other when worn. It's also a great quick knit for a last minute gift!

Sizing

Gauge
22 sts and 32 rows to 4 in. (10 cm) over St st

Finished dimensions
2½ x 3¼ in.
(6.25 x 8.25 cm);
to fit 0-6 months

Materials

- Cascade 220 Superwash Sport, 100% superwash merino wool. 1.75 oz (50 g), 136 yds (125 m) 1 skein in each of the following shades:
  A; 1940, Peach
  B; 820, Lemon

Needles and Notions

- US 3 (3.25 mm) knitting needles
- US 5 (3.75 mm) knitting needles
- Tapestry needle

Instructions (make 2)

With A and US 3 (3.25 mm) needles, cast on 28 sts.
Work k1, p1 rib for 8 rows.
Change to US 5 (3.75 mm) needles and working in St st, follow the Right Duck Chart.
Continue in plain St st for the remainder of sts after the chart pattern.

Next row: k2tog to end. (14 sts)
Next row: purl.
Next row: k2tog to end. (7 sts)

Break yarn leaving a long tail for sewing up.
Thread yarn through remaining 7 sts and pull closed.
Weave in all loose ends and Kitchener stitch the mitten closed.
Block to finished dimensions.
Make a second mitten following the Left Duck Chart.

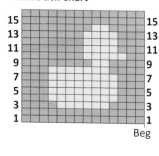

Left Duck Chart

Right Duck Chart

Yarn
A B

Stitches
RS: k, WS: p

Stranded Knitting

STRANDED KNITTING INCORPORATES COLOR BY STRANDING OR FLOATING DIFFERENT COLORS OF YARN ACROSS THE BACK, CREATING AN EXTRA THICK AND WARM FABRIC. IT OFTEN USES COLOR CHARTS, ONLY TWO COLORS PER ROW, AND USUALLY FEATURES SMALL PATTERN REPEATS ACROSS THE ROW. BECAUSE OF ITS EXTRA BULKINESS, STRANDED KNITTING IS STIFFER THAN PLAIN STOCKINETTE, BUT MAKES A MUCH WARMER GARMENT. STRANDED KNITTING IS GREAT FOR ADDING COLOR PATTERNS TO SWEATERS, BAGS, GLOVES, HATS, AND OTHER KNITTING WHERE THE BACK IS HIDDEN ON THE INSIDE.

The most well known type of stranded knitting is Fair Isle knitting, named after the island off the coast of Scotland where it originated. Stranded knitting is often referred to as Fair Isle knitting, but they are not the same. Fair Isle uses traditional patterns and colors, generally "X" and "O" motifs, whereas stranded knitting refers to any type of knitting where the unused yarn is carried or stranded in the back until it's needed.

Tips

- Don't float more than 1 in. (2.5 cm) of yarn at a time. Catch longer floats in the center of the next row, or weave in as you go.
- Carry repeat colors up the rows instead of breaking and joining for each row.

Step-by-step

There are a few ways to hold two colors of yarn while knitting that will help make it faster to knit. Try them out to find which one is most comfortable for you. It will feel clumsy at first but, as with anything, practice, practice, practice, and you'll get the hang of it.

Another tactic used in stranded knitting to help your work move faster is to incorporate steeks. Steeks are extra stitches added to work that would usually be knitted flat, but allow the entire piece to be knitted in the round and then cut open later. It can be an amazing tool for knitting sweaters, cardigans, and more—once you get over the fear of cutting into countless hours of work!

Joining and Floating

1 To join a new color, place the yarn in between the needles leaving a 6 in. (15 cm) tail hanging in front of the work.

2 Drop the old color and twist the new yarn under and to the right of the old yarn, and continue knitting as instructed.

3 Knit with whichever color your pattern calls for first, and when you come to the next color change, floating the yarn on the back of your work. You want the floats to be loosely carried so they don't cause the fabric to pucker.

4 When knitting with two colors at the same time, one color is always floated across the top, and one color is always floated across the bottom as shown. Carrying the yarn this way will ensure the yarns do not get twisted together. You can carry repeat colors up with your work so long as it's not too far a gap between them.

1

2

3

4

Holding Two Yarns

There are a few ways to hold two colors of yarn. It'll take some practice to get the hang of it and be comfortable with two colors. Take your time and figure out what works best for you.

Holding One Color in Each Hand

This method requires you to become an ambidextrous knitter. It uses the Continental method to pick up one color in the left hand, and the English method to "throw" the other color in the right hand, as shown in Figure 1.

Figure 1

Holding Two Colors in the Right Hand

This method is good for English-style knitters who are already comfortable with "throwing" yarn with the right hand. You can hold both yarns over the right forefinger as shown in Figure 2, or one yarn over the forefinger, and one yarn over the middle finger as shown in Figure 3.

Figure 2

Figure 3

Holding Two Colors in the Left Hand

This method is good for Continental-style knitters who are comfortable with left-handed knitting. You can hold both yarns over the left forefinger as in Figure 4, or one yarn over the forefinger, and one yarn over the middle finger as in Figure 5.

Figure 4

Figure 5

Dropping and Picking Up Yarns

You can hold one color at a time and knit as normal, using the Continental- or English-style knitting. Drop the old yarn and pick up the new yarn when you need to change colors. Remember to keep your gauge even when knitting with each yarn.

Steeks

Steeks are extra stitches added to circular knitting and then cut open. It eliminates the need to knit the piece flat. This is especially helpful in stranded knitting because it allows the piece to be knitted in the round, which is the way most stranded knitting is done. Once you have a rhythm going, it's easier to keep knitting around and around, instead of stopping, turning, and reading the chart backwards. Pattern repeats are much easier to remember when working on the right side. Color changes are often done in, or near, the center of the steek so the ends won't have to be woven in because the fabric will be cut anyway. Steeks are often used in sweaters for armholes, neck holes, and even straight down the front to open up cardigans.

The number of stitches used for a steek is entirely up to you. I like to allow nine steek stitches to ensure I have plenty of room to secure and cut my work. You can use a little as three steek stitches if you're feeling confident in your cutting skills. Below is a nine-stitch steek knitted in a checker pattern. Steek stitches can be knitted in lines instead of checkers to help guide in the securing and cutting.

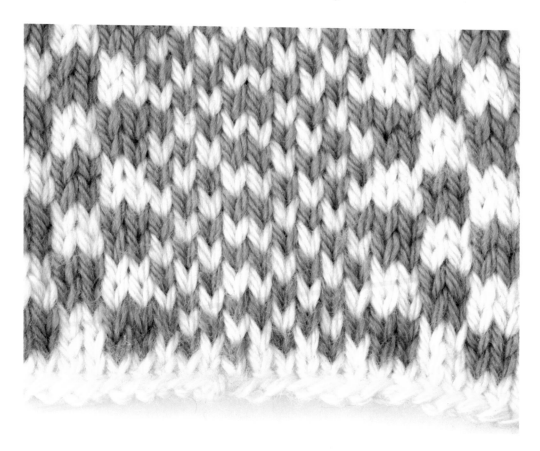

Securing Steeks

Steeks are often secured before cutting, so that the cut ends won't unravel. Blocking steek stitches helps to straighten the stitches for a more precise cut. Three methods for securing steeks are: using a sewing machine, hand-stitching with a needle and yarn, and crocheting along the cutting line. Use a contrasting color yarn or thread so that it's easily visible when you cut. If using a sewing machine or hand stitching, trim off excess steek stitches after cutting down the middle, if necessary. Be sure to use small, sharp scissors to help cut precisely.

Sewing Machine

This method may be harder to do on thicker knits, but will work with finer yarns. It makes a stiffer edge since it uses sewing thread and much smaller stitches. Use a sewing machine to sew two parallel lines down the steek, leaving room in between to cut the fabric.

Hand Stitching

Sewing backstitch by hand with a tapestry needle and a lighter-weight yarn makes a more elastic edge. The lighter weight yarn helps to lessen the bulk of the steek. Use backstitch to sew two parallel lines down the steek, leaving room in between to cut and secure ends.

Crochet

Securing the steek with single crochet stitches is a favorite among knitters. It makes the cleanest cut by binding the would-be frayed yarn right up to the edges of the cut, and creates a nice elastic edge. Usually an odd number of steek stitches are used for this method, because you will cut right down the middle of the center stitch. Use a lighter-weight yarn and a crochet hook one or two sizes smaller than your knitted piece to lessen the bulk. Be careful not to crochet too tightly, as it will pucker the fabric.

To secure a steek with crochet, find the center stitch of the steek. You will crochet along the right and left loops of this stitch, essentially splitting the stitch in half and cutting the horizontal yarns in between. The loops directly to the left and right (half of each stitch) will be also be crocheted together with each side of the center stitch. Turn your work horizontally to crochet up the steek, as you would to work across a row.

1 Begin with the left side of the center stitch, and insert the crochet hook into the loop directly to the left of the center stitch, and the left loop of the center stitch.

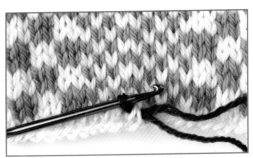

2 Join contrasting color yarn and pull through both loops.

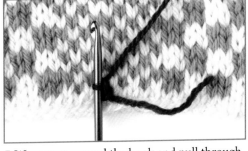

5 Wrap yarn around the hook and pull through both loops to make a single crochet stitch.

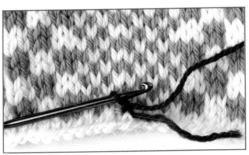

3 Wrap yarn around hook and pull through the blue loop just made, to make a slipknot.

6 Repeat Steps 4–5 to continue making single crochet stitches along the left side of the steek. When you've reached the end, turn and continue as stated for the right side of the steek. The finished piece should look like this.

Stretch the crocheted edge apart and very carefully cut down the center, being careful not to cut into the crochet stitches.

Once the steek is cut, fold back the steek stitches and tack to the wrong side of the work with a lighter weight yarn and tapestry needle.

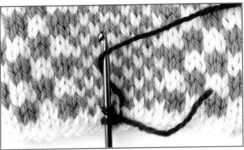

4 Insert hook through the next two loops of the row, wrap yarn around hook, and pull through both loops. There are now two blue loops on the hook.

Designing Your Own Stranded Charts

Making your own chart patterns in stranded knitting can be a fun way to add flair and originality to your knitting. Here are a few tips to follow to help create a smoother knit:

Use two colors per row to make the knitting more manageable. If you're feeling ambitious, and would like to try using more than two colors in a row, hold two yarns in one hand, and one yarn in the other. Or, you can hold two yarns in each hand for a total of four yarns!

If knitting in the round, try to make your pattern repeats the same, or multiples of the same number, so that your pattern is continuous. For example, if you have a twenty-stitch repeat pattern, the ten- and five-stitch repeat patterns will also work in rows above or below it. If you're having trouble evening out the number of repeats, you can center your design and add seeding patterns to either side (see page 98).

Try to keep your color floats less than 1 in. (2.5 cm) apart to prevent snagging and loose stitches. If you want to have longer stretches between colors, catch and weave in the longer float between stitches as you knit.

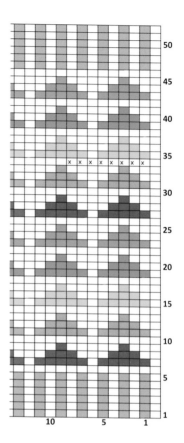

Stranded Knitting

Stranded knitting pulls stitches closer together, and therefore makes squarer stitches than the usual rectangular stitches. Since the stitches are square, regular graph paper can be used to design stranded patterns. Graph paper is available in office and art supply stores, or you can generate your own using a word processor. Alternatively you can use knitting chart software.

Traditional Fair Isle

Traditional Fair Isle uses short one to seven row patterns, known as peeries, that are usually placed between larger patterns. Fair Isle patterns also often incorporate "X" and "O" shapes together within a row, which keep the yarn floats closer together. It also uses allover seeding patterns as fillers, or where shaping is going to happen, so as not to distort the pattern repeats.

Use these examples of peeries to help jump-start your own patterns, and for making deep border designs.

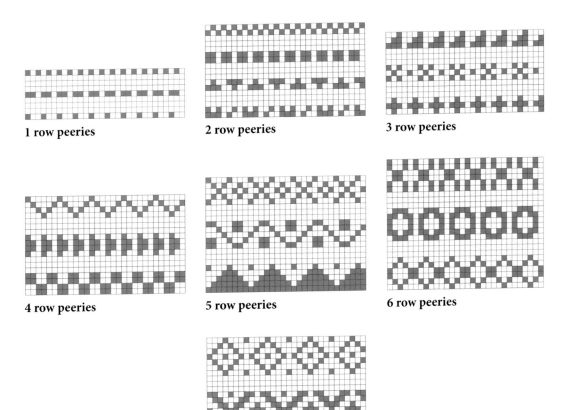

1 row peeries

2 row peeries

3 row peeries

4 row peeries

5 row peeries

6 row peeries

7 row peeries

Try these seeding patterns or create your own:

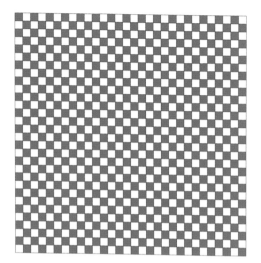 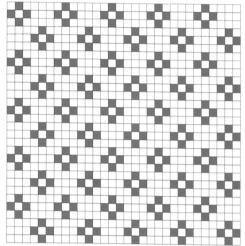

Practice making all-over designs like the ones below:

Fingerless Mittens

These colorful fingerless mittens decorated with triangles will keep your hands extra warm thanks to the double layer created by the stranded-knitting technique.

Materials

- Cascade 220, 100% wool, 3.5 oz. (100g.), 220 yds (200 m) 1 skein A; 8011, Aspen Heather
- Brown Sheep Nature Spun Worsted, 100% wool, 3.5 oz (100 g), 245 yds (224 m) 1 skein of each in the following shades:
  B; N85, Peruvian Pink
  C; N17, French Clay
  D; 305, Impasse Yellow
  E; 131, Lemon Grass
  F; N78, Turquoise Wonder

Needles and Notions

- Set of 4 US 5 (3.75 mm) double-pointed needles (DPNs)
- Set of 4 US 7 (4.5 mm) double-pointed needles (DPNs)
- Stitch marker
- Waste yarn in a contrasting color and similar weight for the thumb hole
- Tapestry needle
- Scissors

Triangle Chart

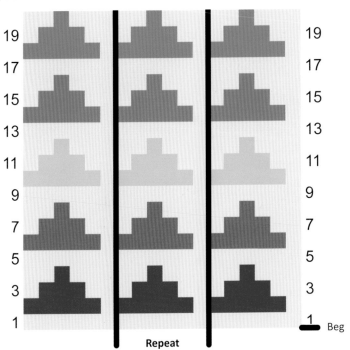

19   19
17   17
15   15
13   13
11   11
9   9
7   7
5   5
3   3
1   1   Beg

Repeat

Yarn
- ☐ A Aspen Heather
- A Aspen Heather Purl
- ■ B Peruvian Pink
- ■ C French Clay
- ☐ D Impasse Yellow
- ■ E Lemon Grass
- ■ F Turquoise Wonder

Sizing
Gauge
24 sts and 24 rows to 4 in. (10 cm) over stranded pattern

Finished dimensions
Ladies Small (Medium, Large)
Circumference: 7 (8½, 9) in./
18 (21.5, 23) cm
Length: 8½ (8½, 8½) in./
21.5 (21.5, 21.5) cm

Pattern Notes

Prepare the triangle colors beforehand. I recommend making yarn butterflies 4 yds (3.5 m) long for each color, and joining the yarn for each triangle color change. In some stranded patterns, if repeat colors are close enough in rows, you can carry the yarn up and continue knitting. For this pattern, carry the yarn up three rows only for each triangle. The distance between the next color repeat is so far up that if you carry it up the fabric will become too bulky.

The Triangle Chart shows size small. The triangle pattern is a repeat of 6 sts, so continue the pattern repeat as required for your size.

Instructions (make 2)

With A and US 5 (3.75mm) DPNs, cast on 42 (48, 54) sts and divide evenly over 3 DPNs. Join for working in the round taking care not to twist the sts. Use the yarn tail as your marker for the beginning of the round.

Work [k1, p1] for 5 rnds.
Change to US 7 (4.5mm) DPNs and work St st in the round (knit every round) following all 20 rnds of the Triangle Chart. Repeat rnds 1-8 of the chart once more.

Next rnd (thumbhole set-up): With A, k1 and measure out 4 yds of working yarn. Wind into a yarn butterfly. You will knit the thumb with this yarn. k8 with waste yarn in a contrasting color, and join A again and continue knitting to the end of the round.
Repeat rnds 10-20 of the chart and knit one round with A.

Change to US 5 (3.75mm) DPNs and work [k1, p1] rib for the last 5 rnds. Bind off all sts and weave in loose ends.

Thumb:
With RS of work facing and US 7 (4.5mm) DPNs, pick up 8 sts directly above and below the waste yarn stitches, and 2 sts at the left edge. Pull out the waste yarn and divide sts evenly over 3 DPNs. Knit in the round using your yarn butterfly.

Rnds 1-8: knit.
Rnds 9-11: change to US 5 (3.75mm) DPNs and work [k1, p1] rib to the end. Bind off all sts and weave in loose ends. Use excess yarn ends to close any holes around the thumb base.

Repeat these instructions to make a second glove, but knit the thumb hole stitches at the end of the row instead of the beginning.

Materials

- Valley Yarns Amherst, 100% merino wool, 1.75 oz (50 g), 109 yds (100 m)
  1 skein each of the following shades:
  A; 91696, Chocolate
  B; 61808, Olive
- Brown Sheep Nature Spun Worsted, 100% wool, 3.5 oz (100 g), 245 yds (224 m)
  1 skein of (C) 131W, Lemon Grass

Needles and Notions

- US 6 (4 mm) double-pointed needles (DPNs)
- US 8 (6 mm) double-pointed needles (DPNs)
- Stitch marker
- Tapestry needle

Tablet Cozy

Keep your tablet snug and protected with this acorn-patterned cozy. It features repeated rows of stranded-knitted acorns. It is worked from the bottom up in the round, with the bottom edge stitched together at the end.

Pattern Notes

Keep moving your end stitches from DPN to DPN to avoid a laddered line in your knitting.
To customize this pattern to your device, add stitches in multiples of 6 and rows in multiples of 7.

Sizing

Gauge
22 sts and 24 rows to 4 in. (10 cm) over stranded knitting
Finished dimensions
5¼ x 8 in. (13.5 x 20.5 cm)

Instructions

With A and US 8 (6 mm) DPNs, cast on 54 sts and join for working in the round taking care not to twist the sts. Use the yarn tail as your marker for the beginning of the round.
Knit 3 rounds.
Rep the 6 st Acorn Chart and work the 14 row rep twice, joining B and C when necessary. Follow the chart for another 7 rounds.
With A, knit 1 round.

Change to US 6 (4 mm) DPNs and work [k1, p1] rib for 1 in. (2.5 cm). Bind off all sts and weave in loose ends.

Finishing
Kitchener stitch the bottom opening closed with a tapestry needle and A. Weave in ends and block to finished dimensions.

Acorn Chart

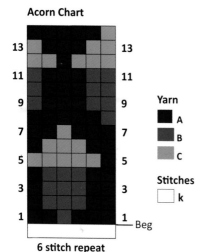

Yarn

■ A
■ B
■ C

Stitches

☐ k

6 stitch repeat

Child's Poncho

This chunky knit capelet is great for kids in the fall when the weather is starting to get cooler. It's knit in the round from the bottom up, and has a fun stranded canoe and oars pattern along the bottom edge.

Materials

- Brown Sheep Co. Shepherd's Shades, 100% wool, 3.5oz (100 g), 131 yds. (118 m.)
  1 skein of each in the following shades:
  A; SS791, Weathered Teal
  C; SS110, Pearl
  D; SS571 Split Pea
  2 skeins of B; SS793, Ocean Floor

Needles and Notions

- US 10½ (6.5 mm) circular needle, 29 in. (74 cm) length
- US 10½ (6.5 mm) circular needle, 16 in. (40 cm) length
- Stitch markers
- Tapestry needle

Sizing

Gauge
15 sts and 21 rows to 4 in. (10 cm) over stranded pattern

Finished dimensions
Child Small: 15 in. (38 cm) long, 14 in. (35.5 cm) collar opening, 35 in. (89 cm) bottom edge circumference
Child Medium/Large: 18 in. (46 cm) long, 16 in. (41 cm) collar opening, 42 in. (107 cm) bottom edge circumference

Canoe and Oars Chart

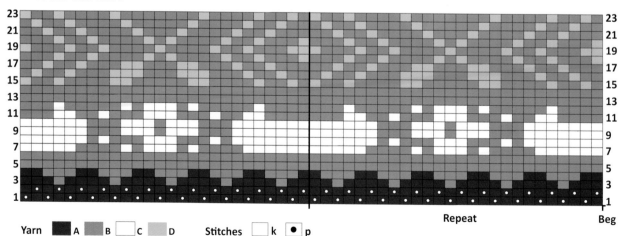

Yarn ■ A ■ B □ C ■ D   Stitches □ k ● p

Repeat   Beg

Instructions

With A and 29 in. (74 cm) circular needle, cast on 130 (156) sts and join for working in the round, taking care not to twist the sts. Pm for beg of rnd.

Rnds 1-23: follow the 26 st chart repeat for the bottom border of the poncho, working in seed stitch for the first 2 rows only.

Continue with B only for the following rounds and change to the 16 in. (40 cm) circular needles when necessary.

Rnd 24: knit.

Rnd 25: [k26, pm] rep to end.

Rnd 26: [k to 2 sts before marker, k2tog] rep to end. (5 (6) sts decreased)

Rnds 27 and 28: knit.

Small Size

Rnds 29-37: rep Rnds 26-28 another 3 times.

Rnd 38: rep Rnd 26.

Rnd 39: knit.

Rnds 40-49: rep Rnds 38 and 39 another 5 times.

Rnds 50-55: rep Rnd 26 another 6 times.

Rnds 56-61: knit.

Rnd 62: join A, knit.

Turtleneck

Continue in A and work [k2, p3] rib until this section measures 3½ (9 cm) long.

Bind off all sts and weave in loose ends.

Medium and Large Sizes

Rnds 29-49: rep Rnds 26-28 7 times.

Rnd 50: [k to 2 sts before the marker, k2tog] rep to end. (6 sts decreased)

Rnd 51: knit.

Rnds 52-69: rep Rnds 50 and 51 another 9 times.

Rnds 70-78: rep Rnd 50 another 9 times.

Rnds 79-84: knit.

Rnd 85: join A, knit.

Turtleneck

Continue in A and work [k2, p3] rib until this section measures 4½ in. (11.5 cm) long.

Bind off all sts and weave in loose ends.

Finishing

Block to finished dimensions and fold the turtleneck down for the collar.

Materials

- Patons Classic Wool, 100% merino wool, 3.5 oz (100 g), 210 yds (192 m)
1 skein of A; 068827, Winter White
- Cascade 220, 100% wool, 3.5 oz (100 g), 220 yds (200 m)
1 skein each of the following shades:
B; 4147, Lemon Yellow
C; 2435 Japanese Maple
D; 9444 Tangerine Heather

Needles and Notions

- US 5 (3.75 mm) double-pointed needles (DPNs)
- US 7 (4.5 mm) knitting needles
- Stitch markers
- 2 buttons, ½ in. (1.25 mm) diameter
- Brown embroidery thread and needle
- Stuffing

Plush Bunny

Handknit toys are so special, and often well-loved. This adorable plush bunny is made with an all-over diamond stranded pattern on its body. The arms and legs are knit separately and attached at the end.

Sizing

Gauge
22 sts and 24 rows to 4 in. (10 cm) over stranded pattern

Finished dimensions
13 in. (33 cm) tall, 4½ in. (11.5 cm) wide at belly

Pattern Notes

Knitted toys are made on smaller needles for a tighter gauge so they don't stretch out when stuffed.

Instructions

The butt, belly, and head of the bunny is knit bottom up in one piece.

With US 5 (3.75 mm) DPNs, and A, cast on 7sts. Divide over 3 needles. Join for working in the round taking care not to twist the sts and use the yarn tail as your marker for the beginning of the round.

Butt
Rnds 1 and 3: knit.
Rnd 2: [k1, m1, pm] rep to end. (14 sts)
Rnd 4: [k to 1 st before marker, m1, sm] rep to end. (7 sts increased)
Rnd 5: knit.
Rnds 6-19: Rep Rnds 4 and 5 7 times. (70 sts)
Rnds 20-21: purl and remove markers as you come to them.

Belly

Rnds 22-46: Join B to begin the 10 st repeat Belly Chart. Work the 10-row repeat twice, and then Rows 1-5 only again.

Head

Rnds 47-48: Join A, purl.
Rnds 49-57: knit.
Rnd 58: [k10, pm] rep to end.
Rnd 59: [k to 2 sts before marker, k2tog, sm] rep to end. (7 sts decreased)
Rnd 60: knit.
Begin to stuff with stuffing, and continue stuffing to the end. At this point, you can lightly block the body by spritzing it with water while it's stuffed, to relax the stitches.
Rep Rnds 59 and 60 8 more times.
Break yarn and thread through remaining 7 sts. Pull tight, secure yarn on WS of fabric.

Ears (make 2)

With US 7 (4.5 mm) needles, pick up 5 sts 1 in. (2.5 cm) to the left of the center top hole of the head. Join A and k 5 rows.
Row 6: k1, m1, k to last st, m1, k1.

(2 sts increased)
Row 7: knit.
Rows 8-11: rep Rows 6 and 7 twice.
Row 12: rep Row 6.
Rows 13-31: knit.
Row 32: k1, ssk, k to last 3 sts, k2tog, k1. (2 sts decreased)
Row 33: knit.
Rep Rows 32 and 33 another 3 times.
Bind off all sts and weave in loose ends.
Pinch the ear together 1 in. (2.5 cm) from the top and stitch together.

Arms (make 2)

With A and US 5 (3.75 mm) DPNs, cast on 18 sts Divide evenly 3 DPNs. Join for working in the round taking care not to twist the sts and use the yarn tail as your marker for the beginning of the round.
Knit 2½ in. (6.5 cm).
Rnd 1: [k4, k2tog] rep to end. (3 sts decreased)
Rnd 2: knit.
Rep Rnds 1 and 2 another 4 times, decreasing the k4 by 1 st on each following decrease round, ending with 6 sts on the needles.

Break yarn leaving a long tail for sewing up, stuff the arm lightly and thread the yarn tail through the 6 sts and pull closed. Secure yarn and weave in loose ends.
Stitch arms to either side of the head just below the purl ridge.

Legs (make 2)

Follow the instructions for the arms, but knit 3½ in. (9 cm) before decreasing.
Stitch to either side of the center hole of the bottom of the bunny. Weave in loose ends.

Face

Stitch the button eyes onto the face with matching thread. Cut 4 strands of brown embroidery thread 3¼ in. (8.5 cm) long and make a knot at the center. Stitch the center knot to the face, making the nose. Use a running stitch to embroider a smiling mouth.

Repeat

Yarn
☐ B
■ C
▨ D

Stitches
☐ k

Beg

Baby Sweater

Wrap up little bundles of joy in this vintage-inspired baby Fair Isle sweater. It features little fawns across the chest, and a heart at the center back for the 3-6 and 9-12 month sizes. Small dots of seed stitches cover the tummy and arms, making it an extra warm fabric all over.

Materials

- Cascade 220 Superwash Sport, 100% superwash merino wool 1.75 oz (50 g), 136 yds (125 m) 2 (2, 2) skeins of A; 817, Aran
- 1 (1, 1) skein of each in the following shades:
  B; 802, Green Apple
  C; 894, Strawberry Cream

Needles and Notions

- US 5 (3.75 mm) circular needle, 16 in. (40 cm) length
  US 6, (4 mm) circular needle, 16 in. (40 cm) length
  US 6, (4 mm) circular needle, 24 in. (60 cm) length
- US 5 (3.75 mm) double-pointed needles (DPNs)
- US 6 (4 mm) double-pointed needles (DPNs)
- Contrasting color yarn in a lighter weight for steek
- F/4 (3.5mm) crochet hook for steek (optional)
- Small sharp scissors
- Tapestry needle
- Stitch marker
- 4 stitch holders
- 6-8 buttons

Pattern Notes

This baby sweater is knit from the bottom up in the round and includes 9 sts for the steek in the cast on and row counts. I like securing my steeks with a crochet edge because it makes a neater edge when cut, but feel free to use whichever method you prefer (see pages 92–95). The steeks are placed between two stitch markers and you should introduce new colors near the center of the steek to avoid weaving in those tails in the end. If you're new to steeking, this is a great beginner piece because it's small.

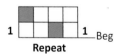

Yarn   A ■ B   □ C

Stitches □ k

Chart A

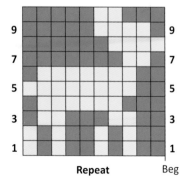

Repeat

Chart B

Sizing

Gauge:
24 sts and 24 rows to 4 in. (10 cm) over stranded pattern on US 6 (4 mm) needles

Finished sizes:
3-6 (6-9, 9-12) months

Finished measurements:
Chest circumference;
20 (21, 22) in. /
51 (53.5, 56) cm

Instructions

Body

With US 5 (3.75 mm) 16 in. (40 cm) circular needles and A, cast on 129 (217, 229) sts. Join for working in the round taking care not to twist the sts and pm for beg of rnd.

Work Rnd 1 in [k1, p1] rib to the last 9 sts, pm, k9.
Rep last rnd another 6 times slipping the markers as you come to them. To help accurately guide your steek later, you may want to use a length of yarn B and begin knitting 4 contrasting stripes (every other stitch) in the 9 st steek section.

Change to US 6 (4 mm) 16 in. (40 cm) circular needles and knit 1 rnd. Follow the seed stitch pattern in Chart A for the Body of the sweater, working until piece measures 4½ (5½, 6½) in. / 11.5 (14, 16.5) cm from cast-on edge. Continue working the 4 contrasting stripes up the steek section with yarn B as set. Leave the Body to one side and move to Sleeve section.

Sleeves (make 2)
With US 5 (3.75 mm) DPNs and A,

cast on 36 (40, 44) sts. Join for working in the round taking care not to twist the sts and pm for beg of rnd.
Work [k1, p1] rib for 5 rnds.
Change to US 6 (4 mm) DPNs and knit 1 rnd.
Follow the seed stitch pattern in Chart A until piece measures 6 (6½, 7½) in. / 15.25 (16.5, 19) cm from cast-on edge.

Attach Sleeves
Starting from the center of the steek, place the Sleeves and Body onto the US size 6 (4 mm), 24 in. ((60 cm) circular needle as follows: 5 steek sts, 25 (26, 26) body sts, 27 (30,33) sleeve sts, place last 9 (10, 11) sleeve sts and following 9 (10,11) body sts onto a holder, 52 (56, 58) body sts, 27 (30,33) sleeve sts, place last 9 (10,11) sleeve sts and following 9 (10,11) body sts onto a holder, 25 (26, 26) body sts, 4 steek sts. (165 (177, 185 sts))

Yoke
Knit 4 rows using the following sequence of colors: A, B, C, B.
Next rnd: k2 sts in B, work 10 sts from Chart B, rep Chart B another 6 (7,7) times, work 0 (10,10) sts from Chart C, work 10 sts from chart D, rep Chart D another 6 (7, 7) times, ending with k2 in color B before working steek stitches. Knit yarn C every other stitch for the steek stripes, lining them up with the previous stripes.
Continue working the charted patterns as established, knitting the first 2 and last 2 sts along the steek in B.

With B, knit 1 (2, 2) rnds.
Yoke decreases:
Next rnd: k5 steek sts, [k2, k2tog] to last 4 sts, k4 steek sts. (126 (135, 144) sts)
Follow pattern from Chart E, knitting the 9 steek sts as you come to them.
Next rnd: k5 steek sts, [k1, k2tog] to last 4 sts, k4 steek sts. (87 (93, 99) sts)
Follow pattern from Chart F, knitting the 9 steek sts as you come to them.
Next rnd: Change to US 6 (4 mm), 16 in. (40 cm) circular needle. K5 steek sts, [k1, k2tog] to last 4 sts, k4 steek sts (61(65, 69) sts)
Change to US 5 (3.75 mm) DPNs and k 1 rnd.
Work [k1, p1] rib for 5 rnds.
Bind off all sts.

Finishing
Armpits
Slip the armpit stitches from holder onto larger DPN, and kitchener stitch the armpit stitches together using yarn A and a tapestry needle.

Steek
Steek the front of sweater using your preferred method and a contrasting color yarn. Be sure to use small, very sharp scissors when cutting for a precise steek. Fold steek stitches back and stitch the edges into place with yarn and a tapestry needle.

Button Band
With RS facing, starting at the bottom left side, using a US 5 (3.75 mm) 16 in. (40 cm) circular needle and A, pick up and k67 (75, 87) sts at the folded edge for the button band. Join A, and work in [k1, p1] rib for 2 rows.

On the next row, work buttonholes according to the size of your buttons by binding off 2-3 sts for each buttonhole. Take time to space the buttonholes evenly, placing the first and last buttonhole closer to the top and bottom edge.

On the next row, continue working [k1, p1] ribbing, using a cable cast on for 2-3 sts over each buttonhole bind off from last row. Continue in [k1, p1] rib for the last 2 rows.
Bind off all sts.

Pick up and k67 (75, 87) sts along remaining steek fold for the second button band.
Work [k1, p1] rib for 6 rows.
Bind off all sts.

Weave in all loose ends and block to finished measurements.
Align buttons with the buttonholes and stitch in place.

Chart C

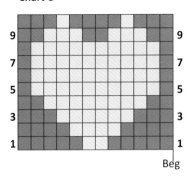

Beg

Chart D

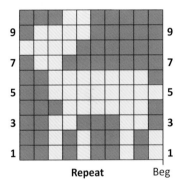

Repeat   Beg

Chart E

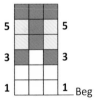

Beg

Repeat

Chart F

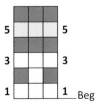

Beg

Repeat

Woman's Sweater

Rows of little foxes sit between stranded patterns in this woodsy boatneck sweater. It's knit in the round from the bottom up and uses steeks for the armhole openings, so the whole body is knit in one tube.

Materials

- Brown Sheep Nature Spun Worsted, 100% wool, 3.5 oz (100 g), 245 yds (224 m), 2 (3) skeins of A; color 144W Limestone, 1 skein each of B; color 146W Pomegranate, C; color N94W Bev's Bear, D; color N91W Aran, E; N04W Blue Knight, F; color N20W Arctic Moss

Needles and Notions

- US size 5 (3.75 mm), 30 in circular needles
- US size 7 (4.5 mm), 30 in circular needles
- US size 5 (3.75 mm) double pointed needles
- US size 7 (4.5 mm) double pointed needles
- Stitch markers
- Tapestry needle
- Small sharp scissors

Measurements

Boat neck opening
8 (9, 10, 10¾, 10¾)"
20 (23, 25, 27.5, 27.5) cm

14 (15, 16, 16¾, 17½)"
36 (38, 41, 42.5, 44.5) cm

7 (7, 7, 7½, 7½,)"
18 (18, 18, 19, 19) cm

13 (13, 13½, 14, 14½)"
333 (33, 34, 35.5, 37) cm

Hip & Bust circumference
32 (34, 36, 38, 40)"
81 (86, 91.5, 97, 101.5) cm

11½ (11½, 11½, 12, 12½)"
29 (29, 29, 30, 32) cm

5½ (5½, 5¾, 6¼, 6½)"
14 (14, 14.5, 16, 16.5) cm

11 (11½, 12, 12½, 13)"
28 (29, 30, 32, 33) cm

9½ (9½, 9½, 9½, 10)"
24 (24, 24, 24, 25) cm

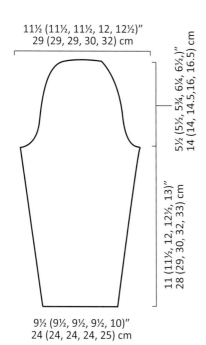

Sizing

Gauge:
26 sts and 26 rows to 4 in.
(10 cm) in Fair Isle pattern with
US 7 (4.5 mm) needles
20 sts and 28 rows to 4 in. (10cm)
in St st with US 7 (4.5 mm) needles

Finished sizes:
Women's Bust: 32 (34, 36, 38,
40) in. / 81 (86, 91, 97,
102) cm

Instructions

Body

With US 5 (3.75 mm) circular needle and A, cast on 190 (200, 210, 220, 230) sts, pm and join for working in the round taking care not to twist the sts.

Work [k1, p1] rib for 3 in. (7.5 cm). K 1 rnd.
Change to US 7 (4.5 mm) circular needle and work Fox Chart until piece measures 13 (13, 13½, 14, 14½) in. / 33 (33, 34.25, 35.5, 37) cm from the cast-on edge.

Shape armholes

Next rnd: bind off 10 sts, work 85 (90, 95, 100, 105) sts in pattern, bind off 10 sts, pattern to end of rnd; 170 (180, 190, 200, 210) sts.

Continue in pattern as follows:
Next rnd: pm, cast on 9 sts for armhole steek, pm, work to second set of bound off sts, pm, cast on 9 sts for armhole steek, pm, work to the end of rnd; 188 (198, 208, 218, 228) sts.

Decrease rnd: slipping markers as you come to them, work 9 steek sts, k2tog, work to 2 sts before next marker, ssk, work 9 steek sts, k2tog, work to last 2 sts, ssk. (4 sts dec) Rep Decrease rnd 4 (4, 4, 5, 6) times. 168 (178, 188, 194, 200) sts remain including steek sts.

Working even until armholes measure 7 (7, 7, 7½, 7½) in. / 18 (18, 18, 19, 19) cm; 172 (182, 192, 198, 204 208, 216) sts.
Change to US 5 (3.75 mm) circular needle, join A, and work [k1, p1] rib for ½ in. (1.25 cm) for the neckline edging.
Bind off all sts.

Sleeves (make 2 alike)

With US 5 (3.75 mm) DPNs, and A, cast on 46 (46, 46, 46, 50) sts, pm, and join in the round, being careful not to twist sts.
Work [k1, p1] rib for 2½ in. (6.5 cm) from the cast-on edge.

Change to US 7 (4.5 mm) DPNs and working in St st continue as follows:
Inc rnd: k1, m1, k to end. (1 st increased)
Work inc rnd every 5 rnds 12 (12, 12, 14, 14) times; 58 (58, 58, 60, 64) sts.

Work even until piece measures 11 (11½, 12, 12½, 13) in. / 28 (29, 30.5, 32, 33) from the cast-on edge.

Shape sleeve cap

This section is worked flat in rows.
For all sizes, bind off 5 sts at the beg of next 2 rows, then bind off 3 sts and at the beg of following 2 rows; 42 (42, 42, 44, 48) sts.

Decrease row (RS): k2tog, k to last 2 sts, ssk. (2 sts decreased)
Repeat Decrease row every RS row 3 (3, 3, 4, 5) times, then every 4 rows 3 (3, 5, 7, 8) times, then every RS row 7 (7, 5, 2, 2) times.
Bind off remaining 16 (16, 16, 18, 18) sts.

Finishing

Block pieces to finished measurements.

Secure armhole steeks with preferred method and cut open. Trim the steeks as necessary, fold back and use fingering weight yarn to stitch to the inside.

Kitchener stitch the shoulder seams 2½ (2½, 3, 3, 3¾) in. / 6.5 (6.5, 7.5, 7.5, 9.5) cm in from the edge to create boat shaped neckline. Kitchener stitch the sleeves to the armhole openings. Weave in all loose ends.

Fox Chart

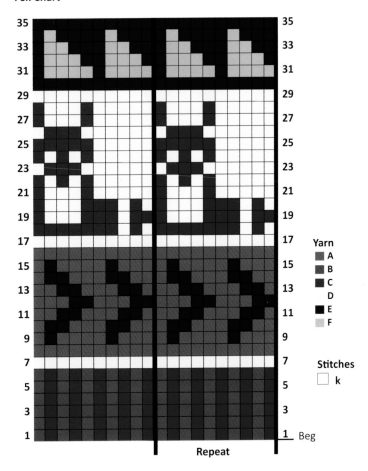

Yarn
- A
- B
- C
- D
- E
- F

Stitches
- ☐ k

Repeat   Beg

Double Knitting

WOULDN'T IT BE GREAT TO BE ABLE TO KNOCK OUT A DOUBLE SIDED FABRIC ALL AT ONCE INSTEAD OF KNITTING TWO SEPARATE LAYERS? THINK CUSHY, SQUISHY, EXTRA-WARM HATS AND SCARVES, REVERSIBLE POT HOLDERS, RUGS, AND MORE. WELL, YOU CAN DO IT WITH DOUBLE KNITTING!

In double knitting, only two colors are used, and stitches are worked in pairs —the first stitch for the side facing you, and the second for the opposite side. Both sides show a stockinette fabric and it takes twice as long to knit, but it makes a thicker and warmer fabric.

Colors can be switched to opposite sides to make mirrored patterns or not switched, to make different patterns on either side. This can make for really fun pieces. Double knitting may seem daunting, but with practice, you'll be double knitting in no time!

Tips

- You may want to use a smaller needle than the yarn label recommends, as double knitting creates a looser fabric. As with any pattern, use correct needle size to obtain gauge.
- Weave in yarn tails using duplicate stitch to hide the tails. Pull the tail in between the work and snip. Pull on the fabric to hide the tail inside.

Step-by-step

Casting on with Two Colors

There are a few ways to cast on for double knitting. These two are used in this book:

Casting on with One Yarn

1 Cast on the number of stitches needed for one side using any cast-on method you prefer.

2 With the same yarn used to cast on, knit into the front of the first stitch, but don't drop it off yet.

3 Purl through the back loop of the same stitch joining the second yarn, and drop the stitch off the needle.

Move both yarns to the back and knit into the front of the next stitch with the cast on yarn, then bring both yarns to the front, and purl with the joined yarn. Continue knitting and purling as stated until the end.

1

2

3

Two-Color Alternating Cast On

This method casts on the total number of stitches for both sides of the piece.

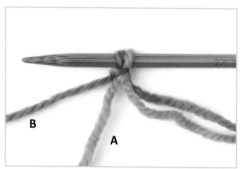

1 With both yarns held together, leave an 8 in. (20.5 cm) tail, make a slipknot and place on the needle. The slipknot will be dropped off the needle after knitting the first row, and does not count as a stitch. Grasp the longer yarns together in your left hand and use your forefinger and thumb to push the yarns apart to make a diamond shape. The yarn closest to you is the front—green—yarn A, and the furthest away back yarn is coral (B).

2 To cast on the first stitch, move the needle to the outside of the green yarn A, and under and up between both yarns.

3 Continue moving the needle up and around the outside of the coral yarn (B), and swing the needle under and up both yarns. This is one cast-on stitch.

4 To cast on the second colored stitch, swing the needle to the outside of the coral yarn (B) and scoop under and up both yarns. The image shows the scooping.

5 Bring the needle down between both yarns and move the needle under the coral yarn (B) and then up, twisting the yarns together. This is the second cast on stitch.

Continue repeating these steps to alternately cast on the number of stitches needed for your pattern.

Begin Double Knitting

Double knit stitches are knit in pairs. The first stitch of the pair is a knit stitch for the side facing you, and the second stitch is purled for the opposite side, creating two sides of stockinette fabric.

If following a chart pattern for a mirrored image in flat knitting, each square represents two stitches—the color shown will be for the first knit stitch, and the second purl stitch of the pair will be in the opposite color that's not shown. On odd numbered rows, read the chart from right to left as usual. The second side will be knit on even rows, use the opposite colors from the first side, and the chart is read from left to right. If double knitting a mirrored image in the round, read the chart from right to left for every row, because you won't have to turn your work. If the pattern has a different chart for each side, read both charts from right to left for each side.

To begin the first row, knit the first stitch with its corresponding yarn. Bring both yarns to the front and twist together to interlock the edge, then purl the next stitch with its corresponding yarn. Continue moving both yarns to the front and back and knitting and purling accordingly. Remember to twist the yarns together after the first stitch of each row to close the edges together. Repeat these steps for both sides of the work.

Designing Your Own Charts

Charting your very own patterns for double knitting can be fun and easy. Since there are two "right" sides to double knitting, you have the choice of making a mirrored image on both sides in opposite colors, or making a completely different pattern for each side. Keep in mind that not all designs will work as mirrored images. For example, the letter J will look correct on one side, but it will be flipped the wrong way on the other. Mirrored, or reversed images, only need to be charted on one side. If using different images for each side, you'll make two charts. Remember that double knitting only uses two yarns, therefore pick two colors that you like together.

Knit stitches are rectangular in shape, so photocopy the knitting grid on page 141, or make one on a word processor or with knitting software, to ensure your chart pattern is proportional to your knitting.

Here are a couple examples of pattern combinations to help your double knitting designing adventures!

Blocks 1 Chart

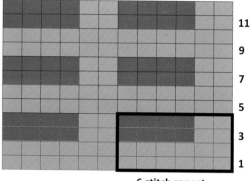

6 stitch repeat

Blocks 2 Chart

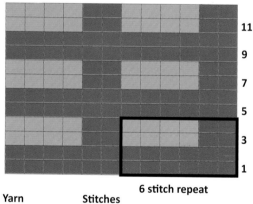

6 stitch repeat

Yarn ■ A ▨ B   **Stitches** ☐ RS: K, WS: p

Mirrored Images

This is a simple block pattern that is the same on both sides, but in reverse colors. Most double knitting charts with mirrored images only show one chart, since the other side is the same, just with the colors reversed. This sample shows both sides for comparison.

Stripes Chart

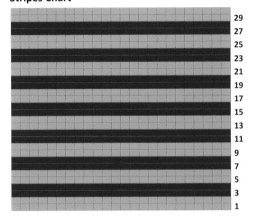

29
27
25
23
21
19
17
15
13
11
9
7
5
3
1

Cross Chart

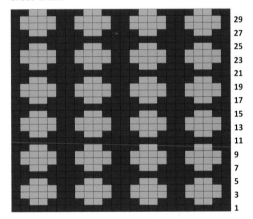

29
27
25
23
21
19
17
15
13
11
9
7
5
3
1

Yarn		Stitches
▨ A ■ B		□ RS: K, WS: p

> # Tip
>
> - If a double knitting chart only shows one side of the colorwork pattern, it means the colors are reversed for the opposite side to create a mirrored image. If there are two charts, one is for each side of the pattern. These need to be closely followed to ensure the correct image appears on each side.

Bird Chart

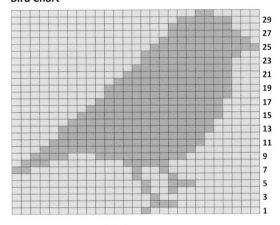

29
27
25
23
21
19
17
15
13
11
9
7
5
3
1

Yarn		Stitches
▨ A ■ B		□ RS: K, WS: p

Different Images on Each Side

One advantage of a double knit fabric is that it has the ability to show two completely different patterns within one knitted piece. Here's an example with stripes on one side, and crosses on the other. Double knit patterns will have two charts if the patterns are different for each side, as shown here.

Motif

A single motif can be added to just one section of a double knitted piece. Here is a bird silhouette that can be placed on one end of a double knit scarf, hat, or bag.

Materials

- Rowan Handknit Cotton, 100% cotton, 50 g (1.75 oz), 93 yds (85 m)
  1 skein each of the following shades:
  A; 335, Thunder
  B; 366, China Rose

Needles and Notions

- US 5 (3.75 mm) knitting needles
  2 US 5 (3.75 mm) double-pointed needles (DPNs)
- 2 (1 in. /2.5 cm) D-rings
- Tapestry needle

Sizing

Gauge
4.5 sts and 6.5 rows to 1 in. (2.5 cm) over double knitting

Finished dimensions
1½ x 46 in.
(4 x 117 cm)

Two-Color Belt

This double-knit belt is reversible and can be worn on whichever side strikes your mood. Use contrasting cool colors like the ones shown here, or pick a pair of monochromatic colors for subtler shades. It's a great beginner piece as it's worked plain on both sides.

Instructions

Using the knitting needles and the two-color alternating cast on method pages 122–123, cast on 16 sts. The number of sts cast on is the total for both sides.

Work in double knitting with A for the first stitch of the pair, and purl with B for the second stitch on odd numbered rows. On even numbered rows, knit with color B for the first stitch of the pair and purl with A for the second stitch.

Continue in double knitting with A on one side of the belt, and B on the opposite side, until piece measures 42 in. (107 cm) or to desired length bearing in mind that the belt will stretch to 46 in. (117 cm) after a light blocking.

Finishing
Slip all of color A sts to 1 DPN and color B sts to a second DPN. Before kitchener stitching together, hold the D-rings on either side of the open edge with the flat side up and in between the DPNS. Kitchener stitch the belt closed with the D-rings inside. It may be a little awkward holding everything in your left hand at first, but thankfully it's a short edge to kitchener together!

Weave in loose ends using duplicate stitch and hide ends on the inside.

Pot Holder

The double thickness of double knitting fabric makes it perfect for pot holders. Keep your hands safe from hot pots with this bumblebee pot holder! This pattern makes a reversible mirrored image, and incorporates shaping on both sides to form a hexagon. Refer to pages 16 and 17 for a refresher on how to shape your knitting.

Sizing

Gauge
15 sts and 22 rows to 4 in. (10 cm) over double knitting

Finished dimensions
9 x 9 in. (23 x 23 cm)

Materials

- Brown Sheep Lamb's Pride Worsted, 85% wool, 15% mohair, 4 oz (113 g), 190 yds (173 m)
  1 skein each of the following shades:
  A; M155, Lemon Drop
  B; M07, Sable

Needles and Notions

- US 7 (4.5 mm) knitting needles
- 2 US 7 (4.5 mm) double-pointed needles (DPNs)
- Cable needle
- Tapestry needle

Instructions

Using the knitting needles and the two-color alternating cast on method on pages 122–123, cast on 26 sts. Remember to drop the slip knot off the beginning of the cast on. The number of sts cast on is the total for both sides.

Knit 1 row in A and, working in double knitting, follow the Bees Chart for the entire pattern. Remember to use the opposite color for the second (purl) stitch of the pair

for the opposite side, so you'll have a mirror image of the bees. Use the left-slanting decrease on the right edge, and the right-slanting decrease on the left edge (see pages 16–17).

Finishing

Slip all the same color stitches onto 2 DPNs and kitchener stitch together. Weave in ends using duplicate stitch and hide ends on the inside. Block to finished dimensions with each edge measuring 6 in. (5 cm).

Chart Note

Each block in the chart represents two stitches for a mirrored pattern. The pot holder is knit flat so on the odd numbered rows, knit the first stitch of the pair in the chart colors shown, and purl the second stitch in the opposite color. On even numbered rows, knit the first stitch of the pair in the opposite color than shown on the chart, and purl the second stitch in the colors shown on the chart.

Bees Chart

Stitches

☐	RS: K, WS: p
M	M1
⧄	RS: k2tog; ws; p2tog
⧅	RS: ssk; WS: ssp

Yarn

▢	A
■	B

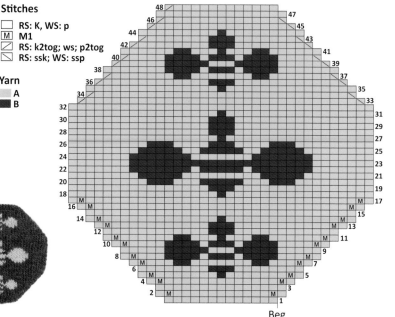

Beg

Double-Sided Cowl

One cowl has two looks with this reversible mirrored pattern. Navy blue forms the background with lighter blue stars on one side, and a light blue background sets the stage for navy blue stars on the other. The darker blue seems to recede, while the lighter blue moves forward. Wear it any way you like for the effect you want.

Sizing

Gauge
17 sts and 24 rows to 4 in. (10 cm) over double knitting

Finished dimensions
19 in. (48 cm) circumference, 6 in. (15 cm) tall

Materials

- Classic Elite Yarns Colors By Kristin, 50% wool, 25% alpaca, 25% mohair, 50 g (1.8 oz), 93 yds (176.5 m)
  2 skeins of each in the following shades:
  A; 3249, Lamb's Ear
  B; 3248, Deep Blue Sea

Needles and Notions

- US 6 (4 mm) circular needle, 16 in. (40 cm) length
- Stitch marker
- Tapestry needle

Instructions

Using A, loosely cast on 80 sts using the one-color cast on method to cast on a total of 160 sts for both sides. Join for working in the round taking care not to twist the sts and pm for beg of rnd.

Follow the Star Chart repeat 10 times around in double knitting, reversing the colors for the second stitch of the pair for the opposite side of the cowl. Rep Rows 1-14 of Star Chart twice, then Rows 1-7 once more. (35 rnds worked)

Finishing
Next rnd:
with A, knit.
Bind off as follows: [ssk] twice and bind off 1 st over the other on the right-hand needle, *ssk, bind off 1 st over the other on the right-hand needle; rep from * until all sts have been bound off.
Weave in ends in duplicate stitch and hide ends inside.
Block to finished dimensions.

Pattern Notes

This cowl begins with the one-color cast on for one side of stitches only, and the second set of stitches is cast on in the next step. Refer to instructions on page 121 if necessary.

Chart Note

Each block in the chart represents two stitches for a mirrored pattern. As this cowl is knit in the round, the first stitch of the pair will always be a knit stitch in the chart colors shown, and the second stitch will always be a purl stitch in the opposite color not shown.

Star Chart

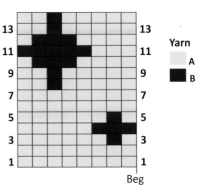

Yarn
A
B

Beg

Reversible Clutch Bag

This is a fun clutch pattern that gives you two bags in one. Pine trees on one side, and stripes on the other. It's a bit more challenging because you'll be following two different patterns for each side, but it'll be twice as versatile when coordinating your outfits! And because it's a double knit fabric, the clutch will be nice and thick, so no there's need to sew in a lining. Ah, the beauty of double knitting!

Materials

- Brown Sheep Lamb's Pride Worsted, 85% wool, 15% mohair, 4 oz (113 g), 190 yds (173 m)
  1 skein in each of the following shades:
  A; M113, Oregano
  B; M120, Limeade

Needles and Notions

- US 7 (4.5 mm) circular needle, 16 in. (40 cm) length
- 1 extra US 7 (4.5 mm) or smaller circular needle for binding off
- Waste yarn to hold sts
- Stitch marker
- Tapestry needle

Pine Trees Chart

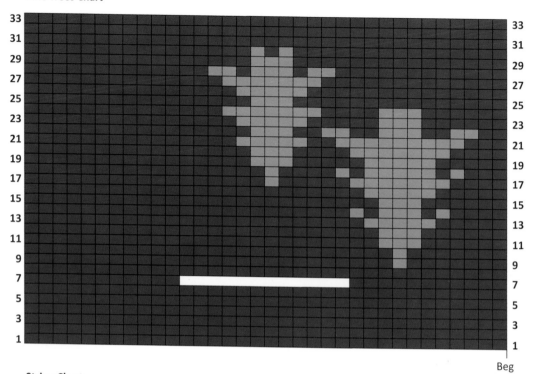

Beg

Stripe Chart

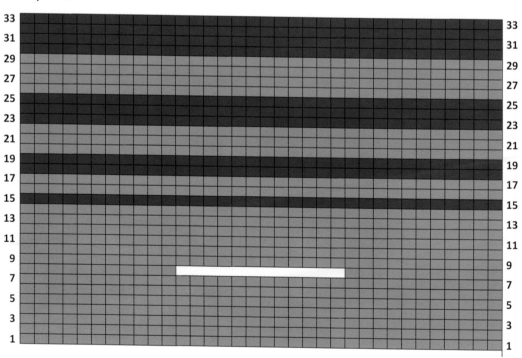

Yarn
- A
- B

Beg

Yarn
- A
- B

Pattern Note

This clutch is designed to look like a completely seamless piece by using Kitchener stitch for the very bottom edge of the clutch and also the top edge of each handle. It is knit from the top down, and in the round. The chart shows the pattern upside down to reflect knitting top down. The handles are basically giant buttonholes and require a little extra work because they're double knit, but definitely worth it in the end.

Chart Note

Each block represents one stitch for each side of the case. As this case is knit in the round, the first stitch of the pair will always be a knit stitch in the Pine Trees Chart, and the second stitch will always be a purl stitch in the Stripes Chart.

Instructions

Use the two-color alternating cast on and cast on 136 sts. Remember to drop the slip knot off the beginning of the cast on. Join for working in the round taking care not to twist the sts and pm for beg of rnd.

Work the chart patterns in double knitting, following both charts simultaneously for both sides of the work. The Pine Tree Chart shows 34 sts for one side. Knit the remaining 34 sts of this side plain in A throughout. Rep the Stripes Chart again after the first 34 sts. Make the first stitch with color A. This will be the pine tree side on the outside, and the stripes will be on the inside.

Handle Bind Off/Cast On

Rnd 7: work 22 sts in double knitting, *divide the next 24 sts equally over 2 DPNs with all the same color on each needle. Break yarns leaving a long enough tail for sewing and kitchener stitch.* Re-join yarns and continue double knitting the next 44 sts in pattern; rep from * to * to bind off second handle. Re-join yarns and continue double knitting the last 22 sts in pattern.

Rnd 8: work 22 sts in double knitting, **switch needles in hands and use the two-color alternating cast on to cast on 24 sts. Be sure to cast on the first stitch in the appropriate color. Twist yarns at the end of last sts to keep from falling off and switch needles in hands again.** Continue double knitting the next 44 sts in pattern; rep from ** to ** to cast on second handle. Continue double knitting the last 22 sts in pattern.

Continue working the chart patterns simultaneously for the remainder of the clutch.

Finishing

Kitchener stitch the 2 "inside" edges and the 2 "outside" edges together, so that the clutch will be able to turn inside out. The outside stitches will be Kitchener-stitched together first, and the inside stitches will be slipped onto waste yarn and stitched together afterward.

At the beginning/ending of the round, use a circular knitting needle to slip the 34 outside stitches onto the needles, and a tapestry needle with a contrasting color yarn for the inside 34 stitches, putting all the same color stitches on 1 needle. If you don't have additional size 7 (4.5 mm) circular needles, use any smaller size. Hold the circular needles parallel to the tapestry needle in your left hand, and alternate slipping the stitches, 1 to each needle. Repeat on the other side.

Slide the tips of the needles to the edge where the yarn tails hang. Tuck all the tails belonging to the inside stitches to the inside. Kitchener stitch the outside edge together with its matching yarn. Turn the clutch inside out and slip the stitches from the waste yarn onto circular needles and Kitchener stitch together. Weave in ends using duplicate stitch to hide tails.

Sizing
Gauge
15 sts and 22 rows to 4 in. (10 cm) over double knitting
Finished dimensions
8¾ x 6 in. (22 x 15 cm)

Materials

- Mirasol Illaris, 100%
  pima cotton 50 g
  (1.75 oz), 116 yds
  (106 m)
  1 skein of each in the
  following shades:
  A; 108, Terracotta
  B; 111, Burgundy

Needles and Notions

- Set of 4 US 5 (3.75
  mm) double-pointed
  needles (DPNs)
- Stitch marker
- Tapestry needle
- Waste yarn

Glasses Case

Slip your eyeglasses into something
more comfortable—or reversible! This
fun eyeglass case has two different
patterns; repeating all-over squares on
one side, and a binocular motif on the
other. This is a more challenging piece
to knit because it has two different
patterns to follow simultaneously,
so keep a close eye on both charts!

Sizing

Gauge
22 sts and 24 rows to 4 in.
(10 cm) over double knitting
Finished dimensions
3½ x 6 in. (9 x 15 cm)

Pattern Notes

This case begins with the
one-color cast on for one side of
stitches only, and the second set
of stitches is cast on in the next
step. Refer to instructions on
page 121 if necessary.

Instructions

Using A, cast on 40 sts using the
one-color cast on method to cast on
a total of 80 sts for both sides, and
divide over 3 DPNs. Join for working
in the round taking care not to twist
the sts use the yarn tails to indicate
beginning of rnd.

The Binocular Chart will be on the
inside and will be all purl stitches
The Squares Chart will be on the
outside facing you as you knit, and
will be all knit stitches.

Work the two charts simultaneously
as follows:
Binoculars side: Purl with A for rows
1-22. Follow the binocular chart for
the next 15 rows, and continue with
A for the next 5 rows.

Squares side:
follow the squares   chart,
repeating rows 1-8 5 times. Knit 2
rows with B.

Finishing
With a tapestry needle threaded
with waste yarn, slip 20 sts of A to
the yarn, and 20 sts of B to a double
pointed needle. Repeat for the other
side.
Kitchener stitch the outside color B
edges together, and turn inside out
to Kitchener stitch color A edges
together.
Weave in ends using duplicate stitch.
Block to finished dimensions.

Chart Note

Each block represents one stitch for each side of the case. As this case is knit in the round, the first stitch of the pair will always be a knit stitch in the Squares Chart, and the second stitch will always be a purl stitch in the Binoculars Chart. The binoculars image will be a reverse image from the chart once turned inside out.

Binoculars Chart

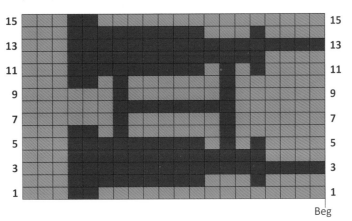

Beg

Squares Chart

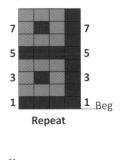

Repeat

Yarn

■ A
■ B

Materials

- Brown Sheep Nature Spun Worsted, 100% wool, 3.5 oz (100 g), 245 yds (224 m) 1 skein each in the following shades:
  A; N03W, Gray Heather
  B; N85W, Peruvian Pink

Needles and Notions

- US 5 (3.75 mm) knitting needles
- 2 US 5 (3.75 mm) double-pointed needles (DPNs)
- Tapestry needle

Pattern Notes

Cast on number is for both sides of the coaster. Each side has 20 stitches that are knit in pairs—the first stitch for the side facing you, and the second stitch for the reverse side.

Chart Note

Each block in the chart represents two stitches for a mirrored pattern. The coaster is knit flat, so on the odd-numbered rows, knit the first stitch of the pair in the chart colors shown, and purl the second stitch in the opposite color. On even numbered rows knit the first stitch of the pair in the opposite color than shown on the chart, and purl the second stitch in the colors shown on the chart.

Coaster

Center your drink on these reversible target coasters. They're a nice small project for double knitting beginners, and make a terrific housewarming gift. And since they're so small, it's a great project for using up last bits of yarn. Mix and match different colors for an eye-catching set.

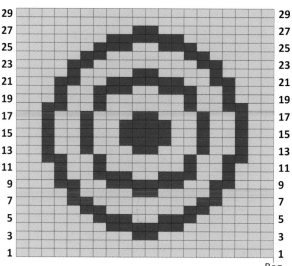

Sizing

Gauge
18 sts and 28 rows to 4 in. (10 cm) over double knitting

Finished dimensions
4½ in. (11.5 cm) square

Instructions

Use the two-color alternating cast on method (see pages 122–123) to cast on 40 sts. Remember to drop the slip knot off the beginning of the cast on and make the first stitch with A. Follow the Target Chart pattern and reverse the colors for the opposite side. When finished, break yarn leaving a long tail for sewing.

Finishing

Slip all color A sts to 1 DPN, and all color B sts to the second DPN. Thread the yarn tail with the tapestry needle, and Kitchener stitch the top edge together.

Weave in ends using duplicate stitch, and block coaster to 4½ in. (11.5 cm) square. Knit 3 more coasters for a set of 4 or as many as you like!

Target Chart

Rows numbered (both sides): 29, 27, 25, 23, 21, 19, 17, 15, 13, 11, 9, 7, 5, 3, 1

Beg

Yarn ▢ A ■ B

Knitting Grid

Photocopy this grid to chart your own designs, or use graph paper for stranded knitting designs.

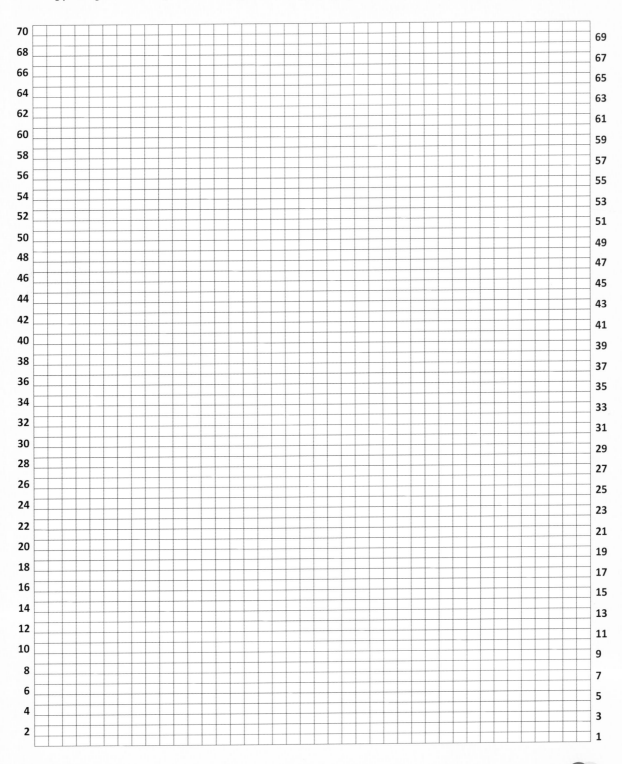

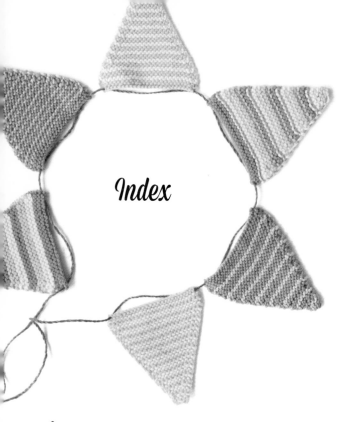

Index

a

abbreviations 11
absorbent cotton 11
Acorn Chart 104
analogous colors 26
Aran 11

b

Baby Bib 36–37
Baby Blanket 34–35
baby knits 10
Baby Mitts 86–87
Baby Sweater 112–115
bar increase 11
basketweave 40–41
Bees Chart 128
Belt 126–127
binding off 11, 13
Binoculars Chart 137
Bird Chart 125
blocking 10, 19
  steeks 94
Bobble Hat 52–53
Bracelet 38–39
brick pattern 50
buttonhole loops 8
buttonholes 85, 115

c

cable cast-on 12
cables 44–47

Canoe and Oars Chart 106
carrying yarn 29
casting off 11
casting on 12–13
  double knitting 121–123
charts
designing 68–71, 96–99
  double knitting 124–125
  Fair Isle knitting 97
  intarsia knitting 11, 68–71
  reading 11
  stranded knitting 96–99
checkerboard pattern 58–61
Chevron Rug 62–63
Child's Poncho 106–107
circular knitting 17
  charts 11
  double knitting 130, 137
  steeks 89, 92–95
  stitch marker 9
  stranded knitting 89, 92
  stripes 30
Clutch Bag 132–135
Coaster 138–139
Collar 72–73
color saturation 24
color temperature 27
color value 24
color wheel 22–27
Color Wheel Cushion 74–77
complementary colors 26, 28
Continental cast-on 13
Continental method 90–91

cord, knitted 19, 64–65
cotton wool 11
Cowl 130–131
crochet hooks 8
crocheting steek stitches 94–95
Cupcake Chart 70
Cushion 74–77

d

decreasing 15
Deer Chart 114
Detachable Collar 72–73
Diamond Stranded Chart 108
double cast-on 13
double knitting 120–139
  casting on 121–123
  charts 11, 124–125
  circular knitting 130, 137
  differing images 120, 124–125, 132–137
  mirrored images 120, 124, 128–131, 138–139
double moss stitch 11
double-pointed needles 17, 19
Double-Sided Cowl 130–131
Duck Charts 86–87
duplicate stitch 19, 80
  correcting errors 93

e

Ear Warmer 82–83
English method 90–91
equipment 8–9
errors, correcting 93

f

Fair Isle knitting 88, 97
  Baby Sweater 112–115
  charts 97
  peeries 97
  seeding patterns 96, 98–99, 112
  steeks 89, 92–95, 115
Fingerless Mittens 100–103
finishing techniques 18–19
Fisherman 11
floating 89, 96
Fox Chart 119
framing knitted artwork 80

g

Garland 42–43
garter stitch 14

brick pattern 50
  stripes 32
gauge 11
gauge swatches 10, 91
Glasses Case 136–137
graduated color 29
grafting 18

h

Heart Charts 72, 115
hexad, color 27
honeycomb pattern 56–57
House Socks 44–47

i

I-cord 19, 64–65
increasing 16–17
intarsia knitting 66–87
  allover patterns 71
  charts 11, 68–71
  joining new color 67
  stranded knitting compared 66

j

joining new yarn 29
  intarsia knitting 67
  stranded knitting 89

k

Kitchener stitch 18, 135
Knapsack 84–85

knit stitch 11, 14
knitting needles 8
  double-pointed 17, 19
  size conversion 8
knit two together 15

ℓ
Leg Warmers 56–57
linen stitch 64–65
long-tail cast-on 13

m
Mail Pocket 40–41
make one left slanting 17
make one right slanting 16
Man's Vest 58–61
mattress stitch 18
Mittens, Fingerless 100–103
Mitts, Baby 86–87
monochromatic color 26, 28, 34–35
moss stitch 11

n
needle gauge 8

p
Panda Chart 85
peeries 97
Pennant Garland 42–43
pictorial designs 66
  designing 68–71
Pine Trees Chart 134
Plush Bunny 108–111
Pocketed Scarf 54–55
Poncho 106–107
Pot Holder 128–129
primary colors 23
purl stitch 11, 14
purl two together 15
Purse 64–65

r
reinforcement 85
Reversible Clutch Bag 132–135
rib stitch 44–47
  stripes 33
round, in the, see circular knitting
row counter 8
Rug 62–63
ruler 9

s
Scarf 54–55
scissors 9
secondary colors 23
seeding patterns 96, 98–99, 112
seed stitch 11, 14, 62
shaping techniques 15–17
single moss stitch 11
slip knot 12
slip slip knit 15
slip stitch knitting 48–65
  brick pattern 50
  color row repeats 49
  knitwise 49
  needles 49
  purlwise 49
  speckled pattern 50, 52–53
  zigzag pattern 51
Socks 44–47
speckled pattern 50, 52–53
Squares Chart 71
Star Chart 130
steeks 89, 92, 115
  blocking 94
  securing 8, 94–95
stitch markers 9
stockinette/stocking stitch 11, 14
  intarsia knitting 67, 68
  reverse 34
  stripes 32

stranded knitting 88–119
  charts 96–99
  circular knitting 89, 92
  color changes 89–91, 92
  correcting errors 93
  dropping and picking-up 91
  Fair Isle 88, 97
  floating 89, 96
  holding two yarns 89, 90–91
  intarsia compared 66
  joining 89
  peeries 97
  seeding patterns 96, 98–99, 112
  steeks 89, 92–95, 115
stranding guide 9
Striped Bracelet 38–99
stripes 28–47
  circular knitting 30
  double knitting 134
  garter stitch 32
  rib stitch 33
  stockinette stitch 32
superwash wool 10
sweaters
  Baby Sweater 112–115
  steeks 92
  Woman's Sweater 116–119

t
Tablet Cozy 104–105
tape measure 9
tapestry needles 9
Target Chart 138
tension 11
tertiary colors 23
tetrad, color 27
tools 8–9
triad, color 26–27
Two-Color Belt 126–127

v
Vest 58–61
visible increase 11

w
washing wool 10
weaving in ends 18, 30
Woman's Sweater 116–119
wool 10
World Map Artwork 78–81

y
yarn bobbins 9, 67
yarn butterflies 9, 67
yarns 10
  carrying yarn 29
  holding two yarns 89, 90–91
  joining new yarn 29, 67, 89
yarn stranding guide 9
yarn tails 18, 30

z
zigzag pattern 51

About the Author

To my ever supportive family, friends, and boyfriend—thank you for always inspiring and encouraging the creative spirit.

Nguyen Le is a designer and also the founder of KnitKnit, an online shop of elegant and witty knitted, felted, and embroidered accessories and knitting patterns. Her work has been featured on the Martha Stewart Show, *Interweave Felt Magazine*, *Knitscene Magazine*, *InStyle Magazine*, *Etsy*, and on various design blogs. She is also the author of *500 Fun Little Toys*, a pattern book using various techniques to make what else, but fun little toys!

Nguyen is from Lancaster, PA and now resides in Brooklyn, NY, where she can be found gulping down tea and knitting out of her pockets.

Websites: knitknitknits.com, knitknit.etsy.com
Blog: knitknitknits.blogspot.com

Some slip stitch and peerie patterns used in this book are common patterns found in many books, seemingly passed around like well-loved folk tales, and others are stitches that I have made up. With so many stitch possibilities, it is likely that more than one person came up with the same stitch.

Suppliers

US

Brooklyn General Store
128 Union Street, Brooklyn, NY 11231
brooklyngeneral.com

Purl Soho
459 Broome St, New York, NY 10013
purlsoho.com

WEBS
yarn.com

Clay Wood & Cotton
133 Main Street, Beacon, NY 12508
claywoodandcotton.com

UK

Loop
15 Camden Passage, London N1 8EA
www.loopknitting.com

Magpielly
magpielly.co.uk

Further Reading

Alice Starmore's Book of Fair Isle Knitting Alice Starmore, Dover Publications Inc., 2009

Color Knitting The Easy Way Melissa Leapman, Potter Craft, 2010

Mastering Color Knitting Melissa Leapman, Potter Craft, 2011

The Essential Guide to Color Knitting Techniques Margaret Radcliffe, Storey Publishing, 2008